Overcoming Your Setbacks

7 Key Steps to Get Past Your Hurdles

Sophia Davis-Fagan

For information about special discount on bulk purchases, please make contact Sophia@overcomingYourSetbacks.com or www.overcomingyoursetbacks.com

Contents

This book is dedicated to my daughter Shanique who I had at 16 and everyone thought it would have been my permanent setback. Instead, Shanique has motivated me to reach for the stars. You are a gift from God!

Acknowledgements

There are so many persons to thank; I am not sure where to start. These individuals have played different roles, and have all contributed in some way in the process of getting this book published. Whether your role was on a large scale or small scale, I consider it to be significant as the book could not have been done without each role and for that I`m enormously grateful.

First, I say thanks to God for allowing me to use my experience to inspire others. Thank you to my family members for your support, my mom Cynthia, Terrence, my children Shanique and Terrence J for whom even at 12 years understands the importance of time management and accountability and did kept me motivated and accountable. Terrence J you are a blessing. My one and only grandson Remone and my siblings Mike, Charm, Christopher and Reinhard, thank you. To my friends who stood by me through it all thank you.

Thank you Raymond Aaron and your team especially Liz who made the process seemed seamless even though it was a mammoth task. To my book architect Rosa and my editor Lisa you are greatly appreciated as I could not have done this without you.

I say thank you to the administrative staff, Professors and all the students from the Global Business Management (GBM) program at Humber College where I was able to learn new skills and to experience what real diversity is.

Thanks to personnel Jennifer, Sarah and Garrett from the Disaster Management department at The Canadian Red Cross for the opportunity you gave me when I needed it. To the management at Walmart Canada led by Payal thank you for the opportunity you gave me at the perfect time. To Bhupinder Singh at Fujifilm Canada, I say thank you, your words of encouragement made a real difference. Brenda Miller, you are one in a million.

My subordinates, peers and management of the Island Special Constabulary Force who allowed me to garner vast experience serving my country for over fourteen years! The experience gained is irreplaceable! Inspector Paul Williams you are special.

My sincere gratitude to Beryl Weir and the Women's Center Foundation personnel who helped me to transition from being a petrified teen mom to an individual who believed that despite my setback the only limits I have are the ones I set for myself.

Last but by no means the least I say thank you to some amazing mentors who have inspired me to take action unknowingly; Oprah Winfrey, Suze Orman, Tony Robins, Jack Canfield, Alvin Day, Robert Hollis, Warren Buffet and Bill Gates just to name a few.

Testimonials

"Anyone who reads Sophia Davis-Fagan's book 'Overcoming Your Setbacks' will be able to utilize the 7 key steps outlined to overcome any setbacks or challenging situations they are faced with. A great inspirational book to read!"

Osmond Bromfield, OD, JP
Chief Executive Officer
National Security Employees' Coop Credit Union
Retired Commandant
Island Special Constabulary Force, Jamaica

"It was an honour to have read Sophia Davis-Fagan's book Overcoming Your Setbacks. It is very easy to follow the guidance of Sophia Davis-Fagan's 7 steps to get past your hurdles. The steps outlined work both on the mind and the body. A must read, as it will inspire you to take action no matter what challenges or setbacks you are experiencing."

Douglas M. Borthwick, Esq.
Attorney at Law
Law Offices of Douglas Borthwick
USA

"Sophia Davis Fagan's book Overcoming Your Setbacks is indeed an inspiring book. It outlines real life and biblical applications to compel readers to move forward, strive for better, and know without a shadow of a doubt, victory is a sure thing despite every challenge. Overcoming Your Setbacks continually reminds us our God is able!"

Rev Dr. Hope McDowell-Gibson,

Senior Pastor

No Limits Ministries International

Canada

"Overcoming Your Setbacks is so much more than a book that provides the relevant tools to transform your life. It gives practical steps which will relief you of your limiting beliefs and motivates you to take action despite the challenges you're experiencing."

Harry Sarvaiya, Broker

ReMax West Realty Inc,

Canada

"Sophia Davis-Fagan's book *Overcoming Your Setback* is an inspirational read for anyone who is experiencing challenges or setbacks in their lives. God has a purpose for each of us and sometimes only with the help of others that you will be able to find it. Sophia's book provides that and more! The book outlines steps you can take to relieve your limiting beliefs and propel you to take action to get you on the path to achieving your goals"

Rev. Pamela Hunter

Pastor

Brampton Church of God Deliverance Ministry

Canada

"Meeting this beautiful soul in 2007, has taught me a lot, humility, determination, courage and success amidst the obstacles. Sophia Davis Fagan is an epitome of courtesy, resilience, brilliance and a passion for serving others. She is a Rogerian by heart, where she believes in the dignity and worth of humanity, no matter what their circumstances are. This outstanding individual has proven time and time again that whatever problems one experiences, there's always a solution. Knowing Sophia contributes to my well-being of humanity, and to serve my community, to the upliftment of others. Her achievements allow me to be determined in my pursuits and continue to pledge that failure is never an option. Sophia's book, Overcoming Your Setbacks is a must read and it is a way of inspiring more people to take action to get past their setbacks."

Jennifer Jarrett, M.Sc.

Guidance Counsellor,

Calabar High School, Jamaica

Foreword

I first met Sophia Davis-Fagan when she signed up for my 10-10-10 Program™ to write a book. I immediately saw the passion she has for helping people and knowing that Sophia was a police sergeant for fourteen years, I said to myself, "Writing a book is a major change for her; a remarkable one for this individual." However, no one is more capable than Sophia to write a book entitled "Overcoming Your Setbacks."

Sophia has obtained a Master of Science Degree in Counselling and Consulting Psychology, and has more than ten years practice as a trainer. She has volunteered her time to coach individuals like you to achieve your goals. She does this by helping you to make better choices to ensure that you experience a fulfilled and purposeful life.

Sophia has experienced her own setbacks and challenges, but she has always managed to get past her hurdles. Not because she is stronger than anyone else, but because she believes that when you're experiencing a challenging situation, there's always the opportunity to learn something! This is the time to evaluate you. Sophia believes that seeking professional help to get you through tough times is the best thing that you could do for yourself.

The seven steps to get past your hurdles, which Sophia has outlined in this book, are practical and very easy to follow. If you are experiencing any kind of challenge or setback in your personal or professional life, reading this book will inspire you to take action.

Sophia's seven steps work on the whole person. She provides you with useful tips and strategies that will help to relieve you of your limiting belief. You know that the mind dictates what the body does, and if you are able to remove the restriction your mind puts on your body then the other parts of the process become easier. This book will put you on the path to taking the necessary actions to move you forward. "Overcoming Your Setbacks" helps you to acknowledge that you have a purpose; it helps you find it and live it.

This book is a must read even if you are not experiencing a setback, because hearing Sophia's story will definitely inspire you to do more than you are doing now.

I encourage you to read this book and share it with your family members and friends.

Raymond Aaron
New York Times Best-selling Author

About the Author

Sophia Davis-Fagan holds a Postgraduate Certificate in Global Business Management from Humber College and a Master of Science degree in Counselling and Consulting Psychology from the International University of the Caribbean.

Sophia has been a trainer for more than ten years. She has a passion for helping people; for many years, Sophia has volunteered her time to help individuals make better choices to fulfill their purposes in life. Sophia believes that in every negative situation there's always the opportunity to learn something.

For fourteen years, Sophia has served her country in the capacity of a police officer and was elevated to the rank of Sergeant of Police. As a direct result of this, Sophia has been nationally awarded the Medal of Honour for dedicated and efficient service.

To contact the author of this book for coaching, training or speaking engagements send email to Sophia@OvercomingYourSetbacks.com or go to www.OvercomingYourSetbacks.com

To My Readers

My book provides you with the basics you need to help you to get through the challenges you are facing. It will inspire you to take action no matter what your setbacks or challenges might be.

My own challenges and setbacks might not have been exactly what you are experiencing or have experienced, but they were hurdles which could have prevented me from moving forward. I could have been stuck like many others who have experienced what I have been through.

However, I chose not to remain stuck; I chose to take action. I decided that no matter what, my eyes will remain on the prize, and that's the goal I wanted to achieve.

You too can take control of your life. It takes courage, persistence and a new way of thinking. You are in possession of all that and more; you only need to look deep within, as they are nicely tucked away waiting for you to utilize them. Just in case you are not able to do it on your own, seek professional help.

"You have a purpose; find it and live it!" Sophia Davis-Fagan

Introduction

"As the reopening of school draws near, she wonders how she will break this news to her parents. The news she thinks will be the most heartrending for her parents, yet, she decided it was time they knew the truth. As the time approaches when she decides to tell them, she was at a loss for words, she just never got the courage. Instead, she leaves home without saying a word, without leaving a note, just to save herself the pain she would feel looking at her parents suffering from what they were about to hear."

That was me! That painted the picture of the setback I personally experienced when I was only 16. Yes, I had a baby. I felt the fear, I felt the anxiety, and all the other negative emotions came gushing down on me.

In my mind, I was finished; my world was coming to an end and I had no future. Moreover, I thought I would be the laughing stock for everyone. It was just thrown away by what I thought was a silly mistake. Would I be able to recover from this setback? Or I was doomed like many I had seen around me? Those were some of the thoughts which were rolling over in my head, with no real answer to them.

As you read through the pages of my book, you will be given bits and pieces of my own hurdles and how I have managed to get past them. You will be feted with stories of inspiration through influential people who have had unfathomable setbacks, but the true essence of this is that they saw their challenges and failures as opportunities to chart a better course, to move their goals forward.

What is your setback? Are you facing an obstacle that you think you will never be able to get past? Or have you been through a situation and you are just not able to muscle the courage to put strategies in place to overcome it? Well, you are in the right place. As you dive in, you will be exposed to seven key steps to get you past your hurdles.

You might be saying, "Oh, many teenagers get pregnant" and, yes, that is true. However, the point I want to hit home is that most, if not everyone, will experience some kind of setback. But it is not the setback itself, but how you react that matters the most. Are you going to sit around and blame everyone and everything for the obstacles you are facing? Or you are going to assess where you are, and see what needs to be done to get you back on track?

You have to take full responsibility for your actions or the lack thereof. Taking responsibility is one of the most important steps in the process of overcoming our setbacks. It is one of the first signs of growth and empowerment. It certainly empowers you to take back control of your life and take the right actions to achieving your goals.

When you are at this stage, you are not only able to continue to push forward, but you are able to help someone going through a similar situation. While I was police instructor, I encountered many of my students who had been through grave challenges, and although they were able to get into training they kept their issues under tight wraps until they manifested in negative ways. However, I was able to help many of them deal with their challenges, which enhanced their chances to successfully complete the training.

Now looking back, I have no regrets as I took charge of my life. I established where I was at the time and took drastic action to start the process of overcoming my setbacks. I totally refused to fall victim to my circumstance as I knew that it would only put me the sea of sameness, which would definitely make it more challenging for me to reach the island of individuality. To see what I have been doing since please go to www.OvercomingYourSetbacks.com.

At the time of writing this book, I am still not exactly where I want to be, but I am very far from where I was at that time. I have served my country in the capacity of a police officer for over fourteen years, and resigned as a Sergeant of Police. For ten years, I have trained police officers and civilian staff members whilst helping others to deal with personal issues.

I am telling you all this because I want to demonstrate to you that you don't have to allow your hurdles to prevent you from achieving your goals. I knew what my challenges were, hence I was able take action.

You too can take action, and you should. You have nothing to lose and everything to gain by doing so. Many times when what we classify as unfortunate situations happen to us, one of the first questions we ask is: why me? I am suggesting that you turn that question around and ask: why not me? You have what it takes to deal with your obstacles. You just need to look deep inside your soul and pull on the strength you have locked within.

Remember I told you earlier that I fell prey to teenage pregnancy. Well, this is a little bit of my own story. I was attending one of the prestigious high schools in Jamaica at the time. My parents had separated, and being an only girl for my dad I was somewhat a sheltered child. I would go between homes. During the week, I would stay with my mom for school as she was the one who pushed for the academics; surprising to say, she had little education. On the weekends I would go to my dad to get money for school.

Like my mom, my dad never spoke with me about sensitive topics like teenage pregnancy. So whatever I knew, I leant from school or from my friends, which was not always the best way. I passed the Common Entrance Examination (a test which dictates which high school students would attend). This was the hardest thing to do as a primary school student, and when you actually passed, you were looked upon as being brilliant (sometimes far from being that).

Your name would be published in the national newspaper, and the bottom line: you were the envy of many others looking on. Looking back, I can now say that was so humiliating for others who were not successful, as their names were not published and everyone would know who they were. Thank God the system has now changed somewhat.

My mother would say to me, "Sophia, no sex until you graduate from school." I dared not ask why was she telling me this at the time, or even to initiate a good conversation about what she was talking about just to ensure we both were on the same page. In my mind I asked myself, "Is she referring to high school or university?" as I was attending high school at the time.

In reality, I knew she was talking about university. However, the topic was so off limit that she did not utter another word about it. That line was regurgitated to me over and over again "Sophia no sex until you graduate from school." Not another word! I look back now and laugh about it; who wouldn't, right? As the book progresses you will be introduced to the 7 key steps to getting past your hurdles!

1. Establish Where You Are
2. Establish Your Goals
3. Invest in Yourself
4. Seek Out a Mentor
5. Don't Settle for Mediocrity
6. Think Big
7. What is Your Purpose?

You will also be given the opportunity to read about 5 influential people who have refused to allow their setbacks to be permanent hurdles. Instead, they have turned their setbacks into opportunity and have become powerful individuals. I hasten to say these individuals were ordinary people in the beginning, but have set themselves apart by the course they charted for themselves over the years.

When you are finished reading this book, you should be inspired to take back full control of your life, despite your situation. You should feel like you can tackle the world all by yourself. Remembering that, in reality, you are never alone as there are many resources out there to help you achieve. You can go to www.OvercomingYourSetbacks.com for more resources.

Additionally, you should see yourself making the impossible possible. And I mean your impossible task could just be taking that first step to get your goals moving forward. Thomas Edison made over 1000 attempts to invent the light bulb, and failed before success came. How many of us could have been able to pursue our dreams with such passion despite so many failures? Certainly not many! This inspiring story is telling us failures and setbacks are inevitable. We should see them as opportunities and never give up on our dreams, at the time we decide we are going to quit might just be the time our breakthrough is imminent.

Chapter 1: Establish Where You Are

Chapter 1.1 Face Your Reality

You cannot change the circumstances, the seasons, or the wind, but you can change yourself. That is something you have charge of. – Jim Rohn

How much progress have you made to achieve your goals? Have you recently done an introspection to ascertain what's happening? When you pretend to have things a particular way when in reality they are not, this gives you a false sense of hope.

It is sometimes wonderful to think about the complete reverse of what's happening in your life. However, the earlier you acknowledge the truth about what's happening with you, the better able you are to deal with it. Not only that, but you will be able to put measures in place to confront the difficulties you are facing more quickly.

Easier said than done, right? It can be done. Many people have done just that and have seen immense results. When you let your failure to face reality get the better of you, it causes you to focus your energy on the wrong things, which in essence lets you lose touch and prolong your situation even more.

Yes, it is perfectly alright to see yourself totally the opposite of what your current situation is. You can temporarily block it out and escape from it. However, your situation is what it is and nothing or no one can start making the change but you.

Rather than living in this fantasy world, begin to see your situation as it is and focus all your energy on strategizing to turn your situation around. Again, you cannot change anything until you begin the process of accepting you for who you are, and start making small incremental changes.

Remember, facing your reality and beginning to change you and your situation are of paramount importance to getting past your hurdles. Stop trying to blame the people and situations around you!

Stop trying to change the people and the things around you and start the process of working on the person you see in the mirror. Yes, start the process of changing you! When you do this, you will definitely start seeing changes happening around you and for you, as you will be tackling your hurdles to effect the changes you want to see.

As Iyanla Vanzant rightly says, "Everything in life is a process. Events occur one at a time until the process is complete! When you are faced with a difficulty in life, the question you must first answer is what is your process? What are the steps you can take to begin working through and out of this situation?" Remember the things you do today will affect your future one way or another, so take responsibility as the lesson you learn from your challenges will chart the course for achieving your goals.

Although it is very important that you face your reality, it's equally important that you do not allow yourself to be consumed by your circumstances. Instead, focus your thinking and your entire being on what you expect to be the remedy to change your situation. In other words, focus your energy on what you want the outcome to be, as it is said that the things that you think about the most are the things that manifest themselves in your lives. Yes, the mind is that powerful and, in practice, we have to try very hard to use it to our advantage.

Chapter 1.2 Take Responsibility

"In the long run, we shape our lives, and we shape ourselves. The process never ends until we die. And the choices we make are ultimately our own responsibility." Eleanor Roosevelt

How often do you blame someone or something for your actions? Assessing where you are in your life is an important part of the process of taking action to move forward. However, taking responsibility is also a very important part of the process of getting past your hurdles. When this is not done, it will prevent you from fully staying on the path to create the change which is necessary to achieve your goals.

That is to say, when you're taking action, you must ensure that the process which is created to get you where you want to go will not be affected by the grudge and malice you might be feeling for that person or thing you feel is responsible for your situation. "Until you are willing to accept complete responsibility for every aspect of your life, your life will keep sending you experiences designed to get your attention." Iyanla Vanzant

It is the norm for us as human beings to quickly come up with excuses when something goes wrong or when life is just not going the way we intend it to go. Do you remember at least once when you came up with a nicely put together excuse when you did not want to take responsibility for something you did or failed to do? I certainly do! The typical one is an excuse for not doing an assignment. I did not have the book. My computer crashed. The internet was down, and the list goes on and on.

When faced with difficult circumstances, it's usually very difficult to accept responsibility for the outcome. Yes, there are consequences for everything we do in life, whether it's good or bad. Taking full responsibility of choices you make gives you the power you need to propel action.

Have you ever gone through a situation that burdened you down so much that you only felt better the moment you began to rationalize it to see what you could have done differently? I certainly have been at that place, and that's when I was able to begin looking at different options.

When things happen to you, it's not the situation which prevents you from moving forward in a positive and productive way. Instead, it's is your failure to accept responsibility and chart the course to redeem yourself. The sooner you do this, the better and faster your outcome.

When you fail to take responsibility for your own actions or the lack thereof, it builds a bad reputation for you. In fact, nobody will want to work or partner with you as there will be a stigma going around with you. This will cause you to lose out on business opportunities or to be bypassed for the promotion you have been anxiously waiting for. It cripples your ability to chart the right path for your own success.

Taking responsibility of what happens to you in life is one of the first signs of growth. It empowers you to take action, people will respect you more, and it builds your confidence and by extension your self-esteem. Accepting responsibility also helps you to rid yourself of one of the most crippling emotions which sets you back, and that is fear. Yes, fear sets people back no matter who they are.

Stand up like the bold person you are and get in the habit of taking full responsibility for yourself and the actions you took which created your setback in the first place. You should all do this, despite the situation, whether it happens in your personal or professional life. In the words of Tony Robbins, "Whatever happens, take responsibility."

- Do you find yourself blaming others a lot?
- Do you procrastinate when you have things to do?
- Do you have a diary?
- How often do you write down the things you have to do?
- Do you write down your goals?

If you answered yes to any one of the foregoing questions please go to www.OvercomingYourSetbacks.com for tips to improve in those areas.

Chapter 1.3 - Don't be a Victim of Your Circumstance

"Refuse to become a victim of your circumstances and give a lift to your potential each and every day against the wish of any obstacle you encounter!" Israelmore Ayivor

It is said that everything happens for a reason. You might not be able to determine why it happened and more so why it happened to you, but one thing you can definitely determine is how you react to it.

You can either be a victor or a victim; which one do you want to be? I am sure we all want to be victors in every sense of the word. But are the behaviours you are portraying indicative of an individual who has conquered his/her circumstances or even wants to conquer them? Are you saying you are not a victim but demonstrating the characteristics of one?

When I got pregnant at 16, I thought no other hurdle could be as high as that one. But I was wrong. In 2010 I lost the only man who ever truly loved me. Yes, I mean that in every sense of the word. I lost my dad suddenly. There were no goodbyes. I was devastated. I was sad and somewhat angry as my dad left without saying a word to me. For months I cried, I could not eat and I lost weight rapidly. I was scrawny. This did not bother me as I was totally oblivious to what I was doing to myself, and did not even bother to think about how I looked. Needless to say, my family and friends were worried about me. I had to do something. Thank God for good friends who never left my side through it all.

I had to look at my life. I finally realized what I was doing to myself and even though I did hold a degree in psychology, it seemed I was not prepared to deal with my own misfortunes. So I sought the help of a psychologist who helped me to deal with it. I had to reposition the relationship I had with my dad. He's not here anymore so now I have to learn to relish the great memories he left with me.

You see, in life we will always be hit with challenges and setbacks, but the important thing is how we deal with them. And even more importantly, if you are experiencing a situation which you are not able to deal with by yourself, it's best to seek help.

Do an introspection too, to see what's happening in your own life. Ask yourself these questions: Am I harboring anger and resentment? Is this worth the time and energy I am giving it? Do I need to reposition my emotional state? If your answers to the questions are yes, you have to find meaningful ways to replace your negative emotions with positive ones.

Do an evaluation and come up with things you can do to rid yourself of those emotions. Tell yourself that anger only makes you bitter and it does nothing positive for you. Try to reposition the relationship you have with the person or thing you are angry with. Get your journal and write down in one column the things which go through your mind when you get angry. In another column, write down the positive things which you can use to replace those you had written down!

What you are now doing is breaking that pattern and creating an alternative to how you will react to the things that make you angry. Finally condition this new pattern by viewing and practicing the alternatives, and in the process of doing this, think about your big why. You are doing this because you want to be happy and live the fulfilled life you are meant to live.

Don't waste your time on negative energy, as it is said that time lost can never be regained! Instead, use your time in a way that you will benefit from it in a positive way.

Personally, my first real setback was becoming a teen mom. At first, I was so ashamed of myself and the wrong choices I made to create my situation. I knew immediately how disappointed my family was, and the unpleasant things people would say about me. I thought my friends would gossip and that they would make my life miserable.

However, I quickly realized that the sooner I started accepting responsibility for my life and the actions I took, the sooner I would start that important process of getting past my hurdles. I realized very early that not focusing on what people thought of me and refusing to blame people for my setback would get me on the path to recovering from my obstacle even quicker.

Think about this, it is said that, "If you can have a big enough reason why you want something you will succeed no matter what obstacles you may face." Or you can have big excuses why it's not possible. But you can't have both." So now as you are reading this, think of your biggest reason why you want to succeed!

Remember I told you earlier in this chapter that refusing to take responsibility will cripple us? This is no different, as when you fall prey to your circumstances, it stifles your growth and development. In fact, this will cause you to be constantly bitter and fearful, and to experience all the other negative emotions there are. This is so toxic that it causes you to always play the blame game, thinking that would make you feel better.

Steps to take to not become a victim of your circumstances

1. Acknowledger there's a situation
2. Take responsibility for yourself and your actions

3. Don't be consumed by anger
4. Instead, be consumed with a new thinking
5. Do constant positive self-talk
6. Surround yourself with positive people
7. Read inspirational books
8. Forgive yourself and/or others
9. Reposition your relationships
10. Seek help from a professional

The victor is deep inside of you. If only you look deep enough, you will discover it. Search yourself, find it and be the person you were meant to be. Nobody says the process of getting past your hurdles is easy. However, you have to be determined and decide that failing victim to your circumstances will never be an option. "Faithfulness imparts God's reason for all circumstances. No matter what the world says, losing is no longer an option." Criss Jami

Chapter 1.4 – Be Inspired by Branson's Story

"You build on failure. You use it as a stepping stone. Close the door on the past. You don't try to forget the mistakes, but you don't dwell on it. You don't let it have any of your energy, or any of your time, or any of your space." Johnny Cash

You have now seen that refusing to fall victim to your circumstance plays a very important part in the process of overcoming your setbacks. You just need to make a concerted effort to not allow your hurdles to impede you from moving forward in a positive way.

You might have heard the stories of these now influential persons who never let their setbacks hinder them from succeeding. These individuals have encountered many setbacks, which for many other persons would have been more than enough reason to do nothing and remain stuck. They could have used their setbacks as perfect excuses not to do well and gradually would have plunged deeper into experiencing anger, hate, resentment and many of the other emotions which come with negative experiences. So now let's look at the story of Richard Branson as told on autobiograpy.com.

Richard Branson, now one of the most influential and wealthy entrepreneurs in the world, wasn't always like that. He struggled academically throughout high school as a result of being dyslexic. Branson got frustrated and decided that school was not for him, and dropped out of school at the age of 15.

Many persons facing this setback would probably look for menial jobs just to get by, but Branson saw it as the opportunity to start his own business. Hence, he stated a youth magazine and several other successful business ventures, which are now called the Virgin Group, which consists of more than 300 companies in several different countries.

You are probably thinking that this powerful entrepreneur has not failed at any venture since his first setback of dropping out of high school. And no, there's no truth in that, as he has experienced failure and defeat in both his personal and professional lives.

An example of this was when his family home of 30 years in the British Virgin Islands was gutted in fire when it was struck by lightning and he lost one of his greatest business treasures, that is, his diary which he took notes in for more than 30 years.

However, this never kept him back as he always sees his failure as an opportunity to venture into something new or rebuild something that is even more beautiful. He rebuilt his home which is now even more beautiful than the previous one. Branson does not harp too much on his failure; instead he focuses on getting better at what he does. This is a great example of a man who has never allowed his obstacles to impede him from moving forward or to even use them as an excuse to not do well.

Branson has indicated to Mark Thompson from the Globe and Mail that the 3 principles that keep him focused are purpose, passion and performance. This does not have to be what keeps you focused. We are all driven by different things and we use different things to keep us focused.

The fact is that we should all be driven and motivated by something, as this will propel movement. Once you start the process of taking action, you will definitely see incremental change.

The most important thing to note about when we experience failures and setbacks is to learn from them, and as much as possible try to turn them into opportunities. "How many people are completely successful in every department of life? Not one. The most successful people are the ones who learn from their mistakes and turn their failures into opportunities." Zig Ziglar

Chapter 1.5 – Make a Journal

'The starting point of discovering who you are, your gift, your talents, your dreams, is being comfortable with yourself. Spend time alone. Write in a journal. Take long walks in the woods." Robin S. Sharma

Do you know how important having a journal really is? For many of us, making a journal is a way of documenting our thoughts and feelings. It can definitely propel our movements forward as it forces us to take action. Making a journal is a way of spending quality time with you. Yes, nothing is wrong with spending quality time with you. Writing a journal has many benefits. Some of the benefits we can get from journalling are:

- It helps us to confront our negative emotions
- It evokes our creativity
- It helps us to be more committed to our goals
- It serves as the first step to taking action
- It serves as a reminder as our brain cannot remember everything
- It helps with our healing process

When we keep a journal it forces us to be more conscious of the things we are thinking about. So let's say that our thoughts are always negative; and we all know that negative thoughts have no benefit to us. Writing it down allows us to see what we are thinking and at what time we are having these thoughts. It basically helps us to face our negative emotions head on and to actively engage our minds.

So now a concerted effort can be made to replace those negative thoughts with more positive ones which we know will be of benefit to us. This also helps us to determine what triggers those negative thoughts and in turn puts us in a position to deal with those triggers to improve them.

How many influential people do we know who have documented what was thought of as simple ideas and later them turned into multimillionaire ventures? Many! Entrepreneurs like Bill Gates, Larry Ellison, and Mark Zuckerberg are some of the people who come to mind. Making a journal induces creativity in us. It brings out our true thoughts and ideas, which if given the focus right will bring a lot of benefit to us; maybe not now but in the future.

Another very important benefit of keeping a journal is that it helps us to be more committed to making whatever is written a reality, especially when we document the little things we want to accomplish.

These can be our short-term, medium-term or even our long-term goals. Writing our goals down, or just about anything we want to get accomplished, no matter how trivial, helps to evoke action on our path as writing our ideas down is the first step in making them a reality.

Making a journal also helps us to remember things. Our brain stores things; however, it does not possess the capacity to give us all the response we want from it. As human beings, we are just not able to remember everything, especially at the time we want it. So writing things down is a great way of backing up our brain, as we can always refresh our memory by referring to our journals. Remember the saying which goes "a pen is mightier than a sword."

Writing about things we are experiencing will help our healing process, whether it is emotional, physical, or even psychological issues we are confronted with. Dr. James Pennebaker, author of "Writing To Heal," has said he has observed improvement in immune function in people who have engaged in writing exercises. He further states that, "When we translate an experience into language we essentially make the experience graspable."

So here we can see that writing things down can be a very powerful tool in all aspects of our lives, and how powerful writing a journal can be. It basically allows us to confront our negative thoughts; it evokes creativity in us and helps us to be more committed to our goals.

This can be considered as the first step in taking action and, yes, it helps with the healing process of most of the issues we face. In the words of Oprah Winfrey, "Writing a journal can change your life in ways you would never imagine."

Chapter 1.6 – 'Do Me Day'

"You give issues, fears and ideas power by virtue of your thoughts. Taking time to pray or meditate is the perfect way to keep your head and mind clear." Iyanla Vanzant

How are you allocating your time? Are you giving your time to everyone else and totally disregarding yourself? If your answer is yes, then it is time you start allocating some time to yourself, and make an effort to implement 'Do Me Day.'

Now, you might be wondering what 'Do Me Day' is. It is a day when you spend your time thinking and doing everything about you. Yes, you focus all your attention and energy on making you the most important person on earth. This is the time when you pay little or no attention to the negative issues and emotions you have. Instead, do the things which enhance you and the goals which you have set for yourself. This time is very important as it is the time when you rejuvenate yourself, so take it seriously.

Many of us spend most, if not all, of our time doing for other people. We literally take on the stresses of others, and that includes our family members, our friends, our work and just about all the stress which comes with life.

Taking on so much stress will drain your entire being; hence, it's very important that you take this seriously and consider this stage of the process as essential as the other parts.

There are so many things you can do to make your 'Do Me Day' what it is intended to be, and to get maximum results from it. And when I say maximum results, I mean on completion of whatever activities you have selected to do, you should feel great about yourself. You should feel rejuvenated and ready to take on the world. Use this time to expand your possibilities and start thinking of ways to live a purposeful life.

Some of the activities you could do include taking a long walk, treating yourself to something special like a massage, visiting one of those friends with whom you could sit and talk about the things you want to take about, watching a couple of inspiring movies or even reading a book.

In addition, you could use this time to think seriously about some of the goals you would like to set for yourself. You might be saying, "Oh but I don't have the money." Sorry, this is not an excuse not to have your 'Do Me Day.'

Your 'Do Me Day' could be once per week, once every two weeks, or even once a month. The most important thing is that you implement this as it will benefit you in the long run. In fact, if you fail to rejuvenate lost energy, you will not be able to effectively help others.

There are many activities that you can do which do not require spending money. Some I have mentioned above. Again, I am stressing the point that there should be no excuse not to spend quality time doing what makes you truly happy.

For example, if you have always wanted to write a book, create a blog or even a Facebook group where you post inspirational information to make someone's day, your 'Do Me Day' is the perfect time to start doing those activities. Why? Because those are some of the things you are passionate about but you just never got around to doing them! You would be surprised at what this simple regular activity could do for you and your confidence level.

Remember earlier I mentioned that one of the activities you could do on your 'Do Me Day' was visiting a friend who usually provides that encouraging word that you would love to hear from someone? It was intentional when I specifically described your friend as one who encourages or motivates, as this is what you want, especially on your special day.

You have to try to avoid people who only bring negative energy and are always looking to bring their problems for you to solve.

Ignore those people totally on your Do Me Day. You have to always use that day to build who you are as a person which in essence will help you to overcome your challenges. I know, like many things, it's easier said than done, but at least try to initiate it even when it is not perfect, because with time everything will fall into place.

The most important thing is to start to implement the change you want to see happening and to place all of your energy on this. In the words of Socrates, "The secret of change is to focus all of your energy, not on fighting the old, but on building the new."

We have now seen that establishing where you are is a very important step in the process of overcoming your setbacks. When you are able to acknowledge your situation and take full responsibility of actions that you have taken or have failed to take, you can start charting the course to getting past your hurdles.

We have seen how Richard Branson, despite being faced with setbacks, turned his obstacles into opportunities, which now makes him one of the most influential and wealthy entrepreneurs alive.

It is also very important that we turn our negative circumstances into opportunities rather than falling victim to them. In doing this, we realize how essential it is to making a journal and having our 'To Do Me' day just to focus all our attention on ourselves and what makes us happy.

You might not be able to get everything perfect at the very beginning; just don't be too hard on yourself as the most important thing is to get started. Mark Twain said it perfectly: "The secret of getting ahead is getting started."

Chapter 2 – Establish Your Goals

Chapter 2.1 Short Term Goals

"If you don't design your own life plan, chances are you'll fall into someone else's plan. And guess what they have planned for you? Not much." Jim Rohn

Are you accustomed to setting your goals? Well, establishing goals play an important part of moving from one point to the next, whether it's in your personal or professional life. Setting goals is a significant component of achieving greater success in anything you do.

Benjamin Franklin says it perfectly: "If you fail to plan, you are planning to fail!"

Short-term goals are the ones which we want to accomplish within a short period of time, usually up to a year. These short-term goals are the foundation to achieving our medium- and long-term goals. Even within your short-term goals, it's important that you set shorter term goals and review them to ensure you are on target. An example of this is planning your weekly tasks, and on Sunday reviewing what you got done, and planning ahead for the coming week.

It is very important that, once we have identified our goals, we write them down. In the words of Steve Maraboli, "If you have a goal, write it down. If you do not write it down, you do not have a goal - you have a wish."

Remember in the previous chapter I told you that writing your goals down is one of the first steps to taking action to ensure your goals are realized. You might be saying that you have no time to write your goals down as it is too time-consuming; moreover, you know exactly what you want to achieve. Hence, no need to get them on paper or on the computer.

Let's do a quick survey! Look around you; whether it is your family members, friends or even your co-workers, the people who usually write their goals down are more committed to getting them achieved as oppose to those who don't.?

The people who usually do not write their goals down complain a lot about not succeeding, not getting anywhere, and blame everyone and everything but themselves.

We also need to be specific about our goal setting. Say, for example, you just left college; one of your short-term goals could be to get a job. In doing this, you have to remember that being specific about what you want to accomplish allows you to implement the most appropriate strategies which will get you to your goals in the time you want.

So now that you have set your specific short-term goals, you want to ensure that you will be able to measure your progress. How will you do that? Let's look again at the example of you just leaving college with the short-term goal of getting a job. You may have written down that while searching for a job you would send out 10 resumés per day. You could measure your progress by keeping track of the number of resumés you send out each day. If you didn't send out 10 resumés, how many did you send; is it more or less? You always want to do more rather than falling short.

Don't worry too much though if you didn't send the number you wanted. You simply have to evaluate to see what more can you do to ensure this. Do you need to manage your time better to ensure enough time is given to this activity? You just need to constantly evaluate what you are doing and tweak your strategies as the need arises.

You now want to ensure that the goals you have set are attainable and realistic. It doesn't make sense to set goals that are farfetched, because no matter what strategies you have implemented you will not be able to achieve them. That's definitely a waste of your precious time. Remember time lost can never be regained so manage your time wisely.

Let's look again at the same example we have been using. Let's say you graduated from college today, and your short-term goal is to find a job tomorrow. In reality, this is unrealistic as there are several stages in the process of finding a job.

For example, you apply, you then will be called for an interview, then perhaps a second interview; there is a background check and orientation etc. So you see it would be almost impossible for you to get a job in a day if you are looking at the normal process to get a job.

Another very important point to remember is to place a specific time when you want to accomplish your goal. This allows you to create and implement those strategies which will aid your goals for that particular time.

You cannot want to accomplish short-term goals and implement long-term strategies. That just will not work for you, instead always place a picture in your mind of the goals you want to achieve and the steps to get you there, just so you will not go off course.

I must admit that even though it was difficult at first, it actually worked for me. After my confused state and the negative feelings I was having, I began rationalizing my situation and realized that my mindset needed to change, and that I needed to get a grip and act fast as I refused to be a part of the statistic of people who have allowed their limiting beliefs to keep them stuck in their situation. As a consequence, I began thinking about what I could do immediately (my short-term goal) to ensure I continued with my education.

Thank God for the Women Centre of Jamaica Foundation; I was able to start the program immediately and continued with my education. The point I am trying to get across is this: the fact that you are experiencing setbacks does not mean you are to give up on your dreams. This is the time you have to double your effort.

Our setbacks occur for a reason; they happen to teach us something. We just have to find out what that is and learn from them. They happen so we can have a story, a story which we can use to inspire others to take action.

So starting now, stop seeing your obstacles as doom and gloom. Take the opportunity today to start taking action. Ask yourself, "What can I do today to make my life better?" Search deep inside as the response you need to take action is just one thought away. "A goal properly set is halfway reached." ~ Zig Ziglar

Chapter 2.2 Medium Term Goals

"All who have accomplished great things have had a great aim; have fixed their gaze on a goal which was high, one which sometimes seemed impossible." ~ Orison Swett Marden

We have looked at setting goals and specifically setting our short-term goals which will ensure that they are realized. Now we can look at setting our medium-term goals.

Like your short-term goals, your medium-term goals have to be specific, measurable, attainable, and realistic. There much be some time attached to achieving your goals. Remember that in setting these goals, there must be a step-by-step plan implemented to ensure you achieve your medium-term goals.

Again, we are going to look at the example we have been using. You just graduated college and your short-term goal is to get a job. Your medium-term goal could be to have the deposit for buying your first car or even a house. You will notice that we did not say your medium-term goal was to buy either the car or the house; it's actually the deposit to secure them. Remember we also mentioned earlier that each set of goals contributes significantly towards achieving the other goals we set.

Another very important part of setting your goals is that they should reflect what you want to achieve, not what your parents or other people want. Often we set goals that reflect other people's interest, or what other people want us to do, which in essence prevents us from putting in the kind of effort required to ensure our goals are met. Your goals should coincide with your belief system, your values and what you believe will be of full benefit to you.

So, as you saw earlier, even though I was experiencing my setback, I was taking action. They were tiny ones, but the important thing is that I was doing something with the help and support of my family. I achieved my short-term goal but I could not stop there as I wanted to get back in the regular education stream. My medium-term goal was to get back in school within one year of having my child, and thank God I did.

Although students at the centre were assisted to get back in regular high schools, I was too ashamed to venture on those corridors, so my parents searched until they got me into a private school I felt a little more comfortable attending.

Again, the most important lesson I want you to take away from this is the fact that I was going through an ordeal; I tried not to think too much about it. Instead, I tried to maintain my focus and planned what I needed to do to move forward.

I was motivated to take action, as I knew that I was now being depended on by another life and there's no way I could let her down. I had to muster the courage, despite the challenges. You too can do it, if only you could see what lies ahead for you, just make that first step and you will have started that very important journey to getting past your hurdles.

Again, don't forget to reward yourself for your achievements even if they are tiny ones. When you do this, it motivates you to work harder at achieving more and in a quicker time. So set aside gifts commensurate with your achievement to keep the momentum going. "All who have accomplished great things have had a great aim; have fixed their gaze on a goal which was high, one which sometimes seemed impossible." ~ Orison Swett Marden

Chapter 2.3 Long-Term Goals

"Give me a stock clerk with a goal and I'll give you a man who will make history. Give me a man with no goals and I'll give you a stock clerk." ~ J.C. Penney

Let's now dive right into our long-term goals. These goals usually take a longer time to be accomplished, usually over five years. Examples of these kinds of goals are buying a house or a car, saving towards your children's education and so on.

Like your short- and medium-term goals, long-term goals require all the necessary ingredients to ensure they are accomplished. You have to constantly evaluate your strategies to ensure they are working as planned, if not you have to tweak or change to strategies which will ensure attainment.

When setting the longer term goals much more consideration has to be given as these usually involve more time and money, and there more to lose if you fail to achieve them.

Notwithstanding this, you cannot give all your attention to your long-term goal and neglect the short- and medium-term goals, as attainment of those smaller goals will greatly assist the attainment of the long-term goals.

Back to our example: you just left college and your short-term goal is to get a job, your medium-term goal is to save the deposit for your first car or house, and your long-term goal remains the same; you want to buy a car or a house.

You have gotten the job immediately so your short-term goal has been achieved. You have totally ignored your medium-term goal and are only focusing on your long-term goal of buying the car. So you are working, your salary is $4000 per month and you say you are going to save 20% of your salary to go towards buying your first car or house.

The first couple of months you have done well. You have saved and you do not touch your savings. Now all of a sudden, you have started to party more, and are buying the most expensive name brand clothes, which now prevents you from continuing to save.

You are still harping on the fact that you want to get the car but you fail to realize that the only way to get that car is to save $800 or more each month. How are you going to attain your long-term goal if you do not ensure the medium-term goal of saving the deposit is realized?

Never forget to celebrate your achievements, no matter how small, as this will boost your confidence to push more to ensure that your goals continue to be attained. Go to www.OvercomingYourSetbacks.com to get simple inexpensive way to celebrate your achievements.

So remember in setting your short-, medium- and long-term goals which you have to consider each as a part of an overall goal. In addition, writing your goals down, as well as the step-by-step strategies you will implement to ensure their attainment, is very crucial to ensuring they are achieved.

You have to constantly evaluate your strategies, and tweak or change them to ensure that your goals are reached within the time specified. It would be nice if you achieved them a little earlier than had planned, but don't be daunted if you fall short this. The most important thing is to keep focused and maintain the right attitude. "When defeat comes, accept it as a signal that your plans are not sound, rebuild those plans, and set sail once more toward your coveted goal." Napoleon Hill, "Think and Grow Rich"

Chapter 2.4 Be Inspired: Story on Oprah Winfrey

"Our goals can only be reached through a vehicle of a plan, in which we must fervently believe, and upon which we must vigorously act. There is no other route to success." ~ Pablo Picasso

In the preceding chapter, you saw how Richard Branson made it big despite experiencing setbacks in his early days. He refused to be a victim; instead, he turned his obstacles into triumphs. Now, we are going to dive into the story of Oprah Winfrey.

When we observe influential people, we rarely see them in any other light than what we actually see here and now. Not realizing that, like many others, they too have experienced more obstacles than many of us could have handled in our lifetime.

The major difference with many of those influential people and others is that failure for them is the time they reflect, learn from their failure and double their efforts to ensure they achieve. Oprah Winfrey is one of those influential people who has turned her numerous setbacks into possibilities.

Oprah's story is heartrending for many, but is an inspiration in itself for many people around the globe.

Oprah was abused at a very early age; she was only 9. She ran away from her home in her early teens and shortly after became pregnant. , . One wonders how she was able to get over these obstacles and to be able to do so well.

It is obvious that Oprah knew exactly what she wanted as a teenager. She moved and began living with her father and was able to begin to make changes in her life. You see when you have the right attitude, and as in Oprah's case a change of environment, wonders can happen.

The important thing is when we are faced with obstacles, even at an early age, it is always essential to assess the situation and see if there are changes that we could make to have a better outcome. Oprah did just that and things began changing.

Oprah did well in her academics and started very early to do what she loved doing: communicating with people through speech and debate whilst working part-time at a local radio station. She entered and won a beauty pageant and later won a full scholarship to Tennessee State University where she continued to do very well in her academics.

Upon graduation Oprah got her first on air gig at a small station in Nashville. She was doing so well and not long after that, a more recognized station hired her as a co-anchor for the evening news.

There, Oprah did not meet the public's expectation and encountered many obstacles. But guess what? Oprah's determination and passion took over. Despite what seemed to be insurmountable obstacles, Oprah stuck with her passion and, need I say, the rest is history.

Over time Oprah has built an empire around media. The host of the Oprah Winfrey show for many years, head of Harpo productions and Harpo Films, as well as O Magazine, and Oxygen Media, Oprah is now one of the most influential women globally. Looking at her, one might think that everything was smooth sailing for her, and that she got everything on a silver platter, but that is far from the truth.

Oprah and her story continue to inspire millions of people all around the world, the majority of whom she does not even know. Like many others, I have been, and continue to be, inspired by Oprah and how she continues to impact the world in a positive way despite her early setbacks.

The learning experience from this is never to give up on your dreams. Maintain your focus, continue to be persistent and keep your eyes focused on your goals. Let nothing or no one distract you from pursuing your passion. Reach for it, it is yours to have! "My philosophy of life is that if we make up our mind what we are going to make of our lives, then work hard toward that goal, we never lose – somehow we always win out." ~ Ronald Reagan

Chapter 2.5 Be Accountable To Someone

"Accountability separates the wishers in life from the action-takers that care enough about their future to account for their daily actions." John Di Lemme

We have looked at setting our short-, medium- and long-term goals and how important it to write our goals down. We have also looked at setting our goals whilst bearing in mind that they should be specific, measurable, attainable, realistic and time bound. Without those factors our goals may never become a reality. Now we are going to look at accountability and why it is also an essential part of the process.

You have to be accountable to someone who is able to measure your actual progress against the goals you have set to ensure that they are on target to be accomplished. That person could be a mentor, a coach or just about anyone who is capable of working with you in that capacity.

You might be saying, but I can't afford to pay to get one of these people. Well, if that is the case, that individual could be you. You should only do this if you are the kind of person who knows exactly what you want and knows how important this is to achieving your goals. Did you know that being accountable is one of the things which sets successful people apart from the masses?

Think back on this: many times goals which we set do not materialize because we fail to put accountability strategies in place. This is often why many persons set the same goals over and over again and they just never achieve anything.

Let's look back on the example we have been using. You just left college and your medium-term goal is to save $20,000 for the deposit on your first home. You started out by saving the $800 per month which was part of the strategy to get to your target. On the 4th and 5th months you have only managed to save half of that which is $400 per month.

Probably you are not even aware that this is what's happening because you lack accountability. So, one accountability strategy could be to do your monthly income and expenditure statement and at least once per month take the time to check your back account statements. The income statement would easily have shown you that you might have increased your expenses which could be one of the reasons your saving of $800 per month was reduced to $400.

You could have easily addressed this by looking to see what you were doing with the money and see how best you could cut back to ensure that you remained on target to achieve your goal of getting your deposit in the time you had planned. So you see how important it is to be accountable to someone, even if it has to be to yourself.

I share with you my experience in writing this book. My 12 year old son Terrence J seriously held me accountable to getting my book written fast. So, when Terrence J didn't see me at my computer, his first question was, "Mommy, have you completed the chapter yet?" When this happened, I had no other option but to resume writing, because I am teaching him that deadlines are to be kept even if you set them to get your own tasks done.

So we have now seen that setting goals and leaving them will not achieve the desired results. We have to put all the strategies in place, and one very essential one is to be accountable to someone. In the words of Bob Proctor, "Accountability is the glue which ties commitment to results."

Chapter 2.6 Celebrate Your Achievements

"Celebrate how far you've come and who you have become. Today celebrate you." Unknown

We are now going to take a look at one of my favourite tasks, and that is to celebrate our achievements.

Of course, celebrating our achievements is an indication that we have seen some positive results; yes, we have seen progress or we have reached a planned milestone. This is not usually easy, yet when we do experience some form of achievement, most times we ignore it and rarely do anything about it.

Celebrating our achievements should be as important as setting our goals and putting strategies in place to accomplish them.

Too many times we see our achievements as nothing, not realizing that we have come a long way and where we are now should be acknowledged and celebrated.

Do you know that sometimes we feel guilty celebrating our achievements? We have made all the plans and have put in all the work needed to ensure that we are successful. We need to stop feeling guilty, and instead be thankful for our accomplishment and consider our achievement as a blessing and an indication that we can now move on to our next goal.

I must confess that personally, I seldom celebrate my achievements, and this is not good for my morale at all. Why aren't we boosting our morale? We celebrate with our friends and family when they achieve, so why not do it for ourselves?

The more we celebrate our achievements, the more encouraged we are to work hard at being successful so we can have more celebrations. "The more you celebrate your life, the more there is in life to celebrate." Oprah Winfrey

Make a pledge to yourself that you will start celebrating your achievements, no matter how tiny they are. The important thing is not how small your achievements are but the fact that you are making incremental steps toward achieving your overall goals.

You can celebrate your achievements any way you want. You could treat yourself by buying yourself something really nice that you can afford, you could treat yourself to your favourite movie, restaurant or spa, or talk to your family and friends about what you have achieved. Remember we talked earlier about your 'Do Me Day'. You could definitely use your Do Me Day to celebrate your achievements. It's all about you, right?

We have seen how setting our goals play a very important part of the process. Breaking down our goals to short-, medium- and long-term goals also helps us to see what we need to do and the time frame within which to do it.

Writing down our goals shows that we are ready to take action. Another essential piece of this puzzle is to be accountable to someone. And we must not forget to celebrate our achievement, no matter how small. "Celebrate what you've accomplished, but raise the bar a little higher each time you succeed." - Mia Hamm

Take a few minutes to think about these, and write your responses down so you can refer back to them!

1. Do you have a plan?
2. If no, what's stopping you?
3. What would you like to accomplish in the short term?
4. What would like to accomplish in the medium term?

5. What would like to accomplish in the long term?
6. If you already have a plan, what have you done today to move your plans forward?
7. How do you feel after doing this exercise?

Chapter 3 – Invest In Yourself

Chapter 3.1 What are Your Strengths?

"Strength does not come from winning. Your struggles develop your strengths. When you go through hardships and decide not to surrender, that is strength." Arnold Schwarzenegger

In the preceding chapter, we looked at setting goals; not only to set them but to make sure that they are written down, and the importance of ensuring that it is done. We learned that goal-setting is the first step in the process of taking action to achieve what has been planned. In this chapter, we are going to look at the ways we can invest in ourselves, and we will start by looking at identifying our strengths.

What are your strengths? You are probably going into thinking mode right now as you are not able to say off the bat what your strengths are. Kudos to those of you who are able to readily say what your strengths are.

Yes, it happens to us sometimes. Someone asks you that question and you are just not able to answer it. If this happens, don't be too hard on yourself, even though it is very important that you know this.

Take the opportunity now to ask some of your family members, friends and co-workers what they believe you are good at. Technology is so advanced now that you can go online and take a self-assessment test to quickly ascertain what your strengths are. Go to www.OvercomingYourSetbacks to find free self-assessment tools you can utilize.

You might be wondering why I would tell you to ask those people that question. But what it does is tease your memory, and put something in your mind for you to start thinking about. Soon, you will realize that you are good at many different things as people have always commended you when you do things. The problem is that oftentimes you brush it off and give it little or no attention. Acknowledging your strengths provides the opportunity for you to build on them.

Often we are more focused on our overcoming our weaknesses rather than building on our strengths. One can never be good at everything, hence focusing too much on your weaknesses will only limit the time you have to build on your strengths.

Everybody has weaknesses and has failed in some areas of their lives. However, the more important thing is use your failures as a learning experience. Don't allow your weaknesses to overshadow your strengths as building your skills, knowledge and talent is a long journey.

Another very important point to note is that it is not to your benefit to pretend to be great at everything, as you will be tested and if you fail, this is where you will be belittled. Surround yourself with people who you can draw on to help in the areas you are weak in.

Your strengths should be your main focus, remembering that those skills, knowledge and talents are what make you invaluable. "In examining the potential of individuals, we must focus on their strengths and not just their mistakes. We cannot be limited by what they may have spilled in the kitchen." William Pollard

Chapter 3.2 How Are You Spending Your Time?

"Don't mistake movement for achievement. It's easy to get faked out by being busy. But the question is: Busy doing what?" Jim Rohn

We just dove in the area of identifying our strengths to be able to continuously build on them as those are what make us invaluable to the world. We also looked at acknowledging what our weaknesses are, but not to focus too much on them, but rather to manage them as much as possible, and to build a team that will be able to complement us in this area. Let's now dig into how well you are spending your time.

Spending your time efficiently by way of prioritizing is one of the best ways to get things done. The way we spend our time will dictate the pace of achieving our goals and the length of time it takes to do so.

One has to make a concerted effort to plan the activities that need to be done, and in what order. Of course, we all know that prioritizing our activities allows us to get the most important activities done first, and the process continues until we have completed all our tasks.

You could get your tasks done by starting off your day planning in prioritized order all the activities you have to do, and trying to stick with it. Make sure you write this down. This could also be done as one of the last activities before you go to bed, as the most important thing is to schedule the activities which take priority. "The key is not to prioritize what's on your schedule but to schedule your priorities." Stephen Covey

Another very important aspect that many of us don't even bother to give much thought to is what we spend our precious time thinking about.

You have absolute control over what you think about, so rather than using your time to think about things which will not be of benefit, find a way to use your thought processes productively. Remember, you are what you think about; our minds are very powerful, take full advantage of it.

We tend to focus our thoughts on negative things, especially when we are experiencing setbacks. Instead, use the power of your mind to get you to the place you want to be, providing you get some action going. It's only a matter of time before the changes will begin to manifest in your life.

Look around you and see how many people you know who are living another person's dream. We could be looking at ourselves, right? Too often our parents, and other very important people we look up to, force us to get into professions and to do other things which they were not able to do themselves.

Usually, this makes us most unhappy, as we have no likeness or passion for it. This is another way we waste our time for many years until we come to the realization that, "I really need to spend my time doing the things which are meaningful and fulfilling to me. I need to find my passion even if it means displeasing the people I love." Remember, there are times you have to do what's best for you; if you are not happy, you certainly are not able to make another person happy. In the words of Steve Jobs, "Your time is limited, so don't waste it living someone else's life."

It takes effort to do the things that will ensure you achieve success. Plan your prioritized activities, write them down and try to stick with it. Take control of what you think about, remembering that you are what you think.

Take charge today. It's in you to be great; you just need to believe in yourself and get started. Once you do, you are on your way. "The secret to getting ahead is getting started. The secret of getting started is breaking your complex overwhelming tasks into manageable tasks, and then start on the first one." Mark Twain

Chapter 3.3 Develop New Habits

"We are what we repeatedly do. Excellence then, is not an act, but a habit." Aristotle

Now that we have decided that spending our time wisely plays a very important part of achieving any success in our lives and we are what we think, we are going to look at how essential is it for us to develop new habits. How recently have you developed one new habit which will benefit you?

Our habits define who we are as they contribute significantly to our behaviour patterns. And that's why it is important to develop those good habits that will contribute to our growth and success.

First, we have to look at what we already have and determine if they are good or bad habits. Usually we have a mixture of both! Once we have determined what habits we have, we then decide on the habits we want to start developing and initiate a plan of action to start the process.

As individuals, we usually find it very difficult to start good habits and sustain them, as we do not start simple and work at improving it by doing it regularly every day. Let's use the example of a person who has decided that exercising forms part of a healthy habit, and that 50 push ups would be a good number to start with.

This would somewhat be unrealistic to begin with, especially if the person has not exercised for a while. In a case like this, it's best to start at a smaller number, say 20 and each day, as you have managed to do that number you increase it the next day until you get to your desired number.

The first number of push ups you have managed to do will motivate you to do more the next time, and the process continues until your habits are developed.

Yes, the process of developing new habits should be ongoing to leave no room for bad habits to be developed, as when these are formed it is usually difficult to stop. In Benjamin Franklin's own words, "It is easier to prevent bad habits than to break them." Again I say to you that when you accomplish any milestone, however small, reward yourself and celebrate your achievements.

Another habit you should develop is to do your monthly income and expenditure statement. And you might be saying "I have no money so I don't have to do this." And you are wrong! No matter how little money you have, you should do at least your income and expenditure statement to give account for the amount of money you received as your income for the month and the amount you have spent. This makes it so easy at the end of the year to do your basic profit and loss statement to be able to measure and compare against previous ones. This is a way of taking action and being in control of your life, Go to www.OvercomingYourSetbacks.com for simple template to start doing your own monthly income and expenditure statement and your profit and loss statement.

When you are building your new habits and you have a break along the way for whatever reason, don't be too hard on yourself and allow that to throw you off totally. Instead, pick up where you have stopped and continue to progress, as once you stop you are allowing yourself room to pick up bad habits, as so many distractions are. And remember bad habits which are developed are usually difficult to stop. "Success is a few simple disciplines, practiced every day; while failure is simply a few errors in judgment, repeated every day." - Jim Rohn

Another way to develop new habits is to surround yourself with people who practice the kind of habits you would like to develop. The reverse is true too; most times when we associate with people who have bad habits we adopt them to really feel like we are a part of the group. "The people you surround yourself with influence your behaviors, so choose friends who have healthy habits." Dan Buettner

"Your net worth to the world is usually determined by what remains after your bad habits are subtracted from your good ones." Benjamin Franklin

Chapter 3.4 Be Inspired by Lebron James' Story

Lebron James was born in Ohio USA. He was brought up by his mom, who had little to offer him as his father had left them. With the help of a coach, he was able to go through school. Lebron had a natural ability to play basketball and it was spotted from an early age.

James's mom had little money; as a result they had to move regularly from one place to another as she wasn't able to pay her rent. It was so bad that he had to be sent to live with his coach who was always helping his mom.

Despite living in poverty, Lebron knew what he wanted and he went for it. Another great point to take note of is the fact that Lebron was making a lot of effort and others saw his effort and helped him along the way. You see, when someone sees that you are making an effort despite your challenges, they are more eager to give you support as they realize the drive and persistence you have.

It's very important that, when you are facing difficulties, you try something, anything, to help your situation, bearing in mind that doing something is much better than doing nothing!

Lebron James continued to perform well at his sport. He copped so many awards and has broken so many records. He signed big endorsement deals including one with Nike for $90 million. Of course when you know what you want, you put your priorities in order to ensure that the more important things are dealt with first.

Lebron could have been like many other boys his age, but he refused. He saw all the negative influences around him, but he set his eyes on the prize. For him, the prize was to be a successful athlete and he has definitely become one the most successful basketball players of all times. He has done so spectacularly that he's now being compared with the great Michael Jordan.

You need to take a page from Lebron James' book. By that I mean, don't allow your temporary setbacks to become permanent ones. Look at your challenges and see where the opportunities are or what you can learn from them, and take action now. You might be surprised that the action you take today makes the difference between you getting past your hurdles and staying stuck in your situation.

Today, Lebron James is worth millions of dollars. Why? Because he put his values in order and is going through life effortlessly.

Chapter 3.5 Educate Yourself

"Education is the most powerful weapon we can use to change the world." Nelson Mandela

In the preceding pages, we have looked at developing new habits and ways in which we can do so. We saw that when we are trying to develop new habits we should start simple and intensify it as we progress through the process. It is also very important that we are mindful of whom we surround ourselves with as we easily adopt bad habits from them. Let's now look at how we can educate ourselves and aid our ability to overcome our setbacks.

When one thinks about educating oneself, one of the first things which comes to mind is going to a college or university. Yes you can attend a university and get an education, but you can also gain valuable knowledge through other means like self-taught education.

Yes, self-taught through the use of technology which is now so advanced, and everything you want is at the tip of your finger.

Whichever way you look at it, gaining knowledge is a great way of investing in yourself.

The important thing is not where you gain the knowledge, but getting the education by any means. Technology has blown the excuse of not having money to get an education totally away as you can access the internet at your local library to start the process of getting your education.

There are so many free online introductory courses that you can access and can take as many as you can manage to take. That's the power of the internet. You can use the internet to your advantage or you can allow yourself to be used by it.

You can also gain priceless knowledge by reading books and getting mentors that you emulate and learn a lot from. This we will look at in more detail in an upcoming chapter.

Education enhances your ability to critically think and rationalize a situation to be able to make an informed decision. Education gained brings about some amount of power; however, knowledge without the right attitude and an effective plan of action is almost useless. So in the process of educating yourself, develop the right attitude; set your goals and write them down and you will definitely be on your way to achieve success.

Another important point to note is that if you have the funds to aid your education, then you can be selective in what you choose to study. You should look at the area of study that will fill the need you have and pursue those courses first. Later, if you so desire and you want to have a contingency plan, you can do other courses that you think you could use as a backup plan of action.

An individual who is facing some kind of setback and has taken the decision to educate himself on the way forward has taken a bold step. This can be the difference between getting on the path to getting past his hurdles and falling victim to his own circumstances.

Take a few minutes to answer these questions, and write down your responses.

1. What's the need you have?
2. How that knowledge you gain will benefit you?
3. Do you have a plan of action?

Chapter 3.6 Create Your Brand

"Your brand is what people say about you when you're not in the room." Jeff Bezos

We are on our way; thanks for continuing the course. We have just looked at educating yourself and how important it is to obtain the right knowledge to help you succeed. We are now going to look at building your brand, as when people see your image out there, they actually see you.

Just like those big names we already know, such as Richard Branson, Oprah Winfrey, Raymond Aaron, Lebron James, Apple, Google and Microsoft, we want to create a brand that depicts who we really are. The moment we hear the names mentioned above, we know what they are known for.

Whether you know it or not, you are already building a brand, especially with the advent and the swell in social media that we all like to use. We have to make a deliberate effort to create the kind of image that we want. Whether we are applying to a college, searching for a job or even if we are already a part of a company, we are always being checked on by different people.

Companies do not want to be associated with anyone who has continued to portray a brand which will damage their reputation or their image. For them, it is not worth it as there are so many other persons on their waiting list who they can call. Your personal brand should be one that you can capitalize on to aid your success.

Social media is a great place to start if you are looking to create your brand. One of the important things you need to consider when trying to build your brand is to be in control of what goes out to the public about you.

It's definitely not a smart move for you to leave your brand creation to chance as that can certainly work against you. There is a saying which goes, "If you're not branding yourself, you can be sure others do it for you." A lot people actually pay Public Relation Officers to help build their brand, but with the burst of social media, you don't have to hire anyone, as it takes just a few seconds for something to become public knowledge. Hence being your own PR will save you a lot whilst you put your brand out there.

Another medium that you can use to build your brand is to write a book. We all have our stories that we can use to inspire others. Again with the advancement in technology a book can be had anywhere you are in the world. When someone hears that you have written a book, immediately he begins to see you in a different light as sometimes people think that only influential people are able to write a book, which is the farthest thing from the truth.

So yes, write your book and use smart marketing strategies and you will build your brand in no time. You will be known as the author who writes the book on 'Overcoming Your Setbacks" for example.

The writing of a book opens up doors that before writing you could never have gone to knock on in the first place. That's the power of writing a book. It gives you power, authority, and increases more avenues for greater success. This you should definitely capitalize on!

There are so many authors out there who have used this medium to tell their story. And guess what, people are being inspired by it whilst the authors are benefitting from this exposure in so many different ways.

One of my mentors, Raymond Aaron, says that one of the ways you can start getting recognition is to write a book. Raymond tells of his own story of being 39 years old, divorced, without a job, and $100,000 in debt. He wrote a book and immediately his life began to change. See more of Raymond's story in a further chapter.

I hasten to note, however, that writing a book in and of itself will not bring with it power, authority and building the brand you are looking for, without you making the concerted effort to market your book. Your book has to be marketed in a way that it sells you and creates that brand that you are looking for.

Start creating you brand. Take control of the brand you want to build or someone will do it for you. Use social media or write a book to help create the brand you want.

"All of us need to understand the importance of branding. We are CEOs of our own companies: Me Inc. To be in business today, our most important job is to be head marketer for the brand called you." – Tom Peters

Write the responses to these questions down somewhere.

1. Do you have your personal brand?
2. What brand do you want to build for yourself?
3. Are you in control of building your brand?
4. What can you do to protect your brand?
5. If you haven't started to create your brand, what can you do today to start?

Chapter 4 – Seek Out A Mentor Or A Coach

Chapter 4.1 Find a Person To Mentor Or Coach You

"Leaders should influence other in such a way that it builds people up, encourages and edifies them so they can duplicate this attitude in others." Bob Goshen

We have just moved on from our chapter on the different things we need to do to invest in ourselves. We talked about ascertaining what our strengths are and building on them, and how productively we are using the limited time we have. We also looked at ways of developing new habits, and the importance of educating ourselves, making the point that college is not the only medium through which education can be had.

Finally, we shared the inspirational story of an influential person who experienced setbacks but did not allow them to define who he would become, and the importance of taking control of the brand you want to be known for. Now we will look at seeking out a mentor or coach to help you live the fulfilled life that you desire.

Your Life Coach Saves You Time And Money

Have you ever wondered why some persons are so successful whilst others are merely living from pay cheque to pay cheque or just stuck in their personal or business lives? The answer is simple; those people have coaches whilst the others do not.

Have a life coach will save you time and money. The coach navigates the way for you and the guides you in the direction which will ensure that it does not takes prolonged time to achieve your goals. Time is precious and it that resource which is scarce and you just cannot get no more than the 24 hours the day already has.

So, it important that you use your time in such a way which will ensure planned results in as shortest time as possible. Trying to pursue your goals by yourself will only lengthen the time it takes for you to achieve them. With a life coach, you can never be stuck as there's always this person to help you.

Think of your coach as going on a journey with a GPS that not only tells you where to go but also shows you the exact way to get to your destination. You see what I mean! So if somewhere were to give you a car and tells you that you're going to X place for a conference and then another person gives you a similar car with a GPS and then tells you where you were going, which one would you have chosen? I am absolutely sure that I would have chosen the option which gives the GPS to show me the exact route. This will save you the stress and frustration of getting lost which in the end will saves you money.

Let's look back at the same scenario we used earlier about the two options you were given. So if you had selected the first option of going to the conference without having the GPS to direct you, then you would have to buy more fuel for the car, more food as you would be lost so many times and need extra things.

In fact, not only that, but chances are, you might miss the conference or be late for it and that would be time lost which cannot be regained. So, you see the stress, frustration and all the other challenges which you might encounter when you try to do things on your own. It definitely will cost you more money in the end. I hope you get the point I am making.

Your Life Coach Gets You Results Quicker

If you should take a look at the big names in politics, business or sports whether it's the President of the United States, Richard Branson, Oprah Winfrey, Usain Bolt, Michael Jordan and all the other successful people! There's only one thing in common which makes them successful; that is, they all have their coaches and advisors who direct and guide what they do. If we take a deeper look at the athletes, as soon as they get themselves coaches, they start clocking better times until they ultimately see the exact results they are looking for. When they were on their own without a coach, it seemed they would never see the desired results. Of course, it's works the same way for you when you get yourself a life coach to guide you. The life coach significantly reduces the time it would take you to achieve your goals if you were pursuing them by yourself.

You might be one of them who say, "Oh, I will never be able to afford to pay a life coach." Guess what, the costs of not have one can be exorbitant, so get one now.

The rules apply if you were thinking of getting a mentor. The mentor you get should be the kind of person who can provide the kind of guidance that you are seeking. There are however, a couple of things that you need to do first before you try getting that mentor.

You first need to have very clear and specific expectations of this person. Not only that but those expectations are to be written down. You want to decide what kind of role this person will play in your life before you actually seek one out.

Now that you have decided what your expectations are and what role your mentor will play, you are going to look around you to see who would be a good fit.

Your mentors can be found in your local schools, or the kind of business or profession you want to get into. You need to schedule a meeting with this individual, and there are many ways you can meet if the person is too busy or too far away to meet with you in person. You could Skype, Google Hangout, IMO, to name a few.

When you meet with your potential mentor, it's very important that you outline what it is you are looking for, and what your goals and expectations are. You both should agree on all the different things you are looking for. Ensure you get confirmation from your potential mentor that they are willing and able to play that role, before you even outline what other confidential things are. If the person has agreed to mentor you, you now need to take it one step further.

You need to ascertain how often you will be able to communicate with your mentor, and the medium through which communication will take place. You also need to always be prepared with the different things you want to talk with your mentor about; never get together with your mentor without being prepared.

Remember, you are trying to get the most out of your mentoring relationship with this person. Another very important point which I want you to consider is that, when you want to discuss or need guidance on a particular topic which you think your mentor might need time to get the necessary information about, communicate this to the individual so they have enough time to get the proper information for you. As time passes, you should be seeing some clear progress.

Again, remember that, when you get a mentor your aim is always to get the most benefit out of it. So get involved, make it interactive, and don't be afraid to ask a lot of questions as in the long run you want to be able to look back and say it was well worth it. "Tell me and I forget, teach me and I may remember, involve me and I learn." Benjamin Franklin

Chapter 4.2 Be Inspired By Other People's Experience

"As we let our own light shine we unconsciously give other people the permission to do the same." Nelson Mandela

We have just gone through finding a person to mentor you and we have said that there are a couple of things to consider before you actually go searching. Let's now look at the point of using other people's experiences to motivate ourselves.

The world around us is a diverse place. There are many people out there who are doing great things. To be inspired by other people's experiences, you have to connect with them in some way.

Of course, I'm not saying that you are to jet around the world to connect with people. All I am simply saying is that you have to know what their stories are about, and there are many different ways of learning about people and their experiences. You can read books that provide information about them, or you can use social media and the internet in general, as this is the fastest way to get information about everything. You can simple google the name of the persons you are interested in, and in seconds information pops up.

It is good when you know what's happening with people as you can learn from what they have experienced. You can use their bad experiences as a guard not to go through the same thing, especially if they have clearly stated what those setbacks are. There might be times when you are going through some challenging situation and you feel that you are alone, like it is unique to you, when in fact others have experienced the same thing.

When you can actually read or watch someone telling you that they've been at the place you are at, it makes you realize that you are not alone. However, the major difference is that they never allowed it to conquer them.

Instead, they use it as a learning experience, and that only motivates them more not to give in or become victim of their circumstances. When you can relate to what someone else has been through it should motivate you to take action because if that person is able to get past their hurdle, you should be able to do it too. It all comes down to how badly you want to achieve. You should be so inspired that failure in your head is nonexistent; it is just not an option for you.

Of course, in your quest to be inspired by other people's experiences, be mindful of what you fill your mind with as you do not want to be consumed by too much negativity; just to be inspired by someone else's experience. Remember the saying, "Energy goes where focus goes."

Also remember that being inspired by other people's experiences alone will not move you forward; you have to take action. And I mean you have to make a conscious effort to take action. No matter what you are thinking and doing, if you are not taking action, you are going to be stuck in your situation.

For those of us who are Christians and look to God for that divine intervention, wake up and take charge of your life. Don't sit around and do nothing believing that God is going to literally move you from one place to the next. Yes, miracles do happen, but remember God helps those who help themselves. So align yourself in the right position so that God can give you the blessing you are looking for.

We block our own blessing sometimes because of our inability to take action, and we are always in a state of negativity. Another very common thing we do which prevents us from moving forward is watching and comparing ourselves with other people. By that I mean we are not looking to learn or be inspired by the other person, but rather acting from a position of envy. Stop doing that; there is no benefit. Instead, start focusing your attention on where you want to go and the plans you need to put in place to get there.

Your life depends on you to get up and make the first move. The first step is usually the most difficult one, and once you have mustered the courage to take to take that initial step, your journey will have begun. Once that you have made many steps and continue to make strides, you will be able to look back at the situation, and will wonder what was keeping you back and preventing you from making that first step.

Of course, it's said that people are naturally afraid of the unknown; if that wasn't the case, most people would not have struggles. They would easily see a pathway that would take them forward to achieving their goals.

It's not by chance that I am telling you about other people's stories; it was actually deliberate. When you come to the realization that ordinary people like yourself have had vast challenges but never allowed it to set them back, but rather learned from their situation and continued to take action until their goals were accomplished, it will encourage you to take action too. "Our only limitations are those we set up in our own minds." Napoleon Hill

Chapter 4.3 Read Inspirational Books

"Books give a soul to the universe, wings to the mind, flight to the imagination, and life to everything." Unknown

How recently have you read a book, a magazine or just about any material that edified you? Reading is a great way of distracting you from what you are going through.. It stimulates the mind and allows you think of the unfathomable.

Despite the fact that reading has so much positive effect on us, we fail to read as often as we should. Instead, we get caught up in all kinds of other activities like surfing the internet, watching television, shopping and various kinds of other activities. In fact, if you find that you are not reading as you ought to, you probably need to take a serious look at your schedule and make a concerted effort to set aside time for your reading.

Reading allows you to see the world through the eyes of another person. It takes you to places you may never be able to go in your lifetime, except for using your imagination.

We have no excuse not to be reading as it costs nothing to go to our local library and get literally any kind of book we desire. Another way of getting books is to look out for free e-books which are always been given out by authors nowadays. Basically, you have no excuse not to be reading as there are so many different options.

There are so many other benefits from reading a book. Books help to build your vocabulary. In fact when I am reading a book and come across a new word, I am forced to look up the meaning if it does not readily come out in the sentence.

This causes a domino effect, as what it does is to help you with your writing skills and even improve your reasoning ability and your critical thinking skills. Seriously, have you ever had a conversation with someone and you were at a loss for words? And it's not that you don't know what you want to say; you do, but the word you want to bring home what you are trying to say just will not come to memory. Yes, it has happened to me before and one way of improving this is to read more.

Reading provides you with valuable information and takes away myths which we have in our minds. Take the topic of money, for example. So many people have concluded that they will never be able to have money as they do not earn enough to invest in the stock market and other investment types as it is only for the wealthy people. Wrong!

One of the books I recently read was "Money: Master The Game" by Tony Robbins, and can I tell you that it is a must read for the ordinary person as it provides investment information that you would not have gotten access to otherwise, apart from putting to rest the myths people have about investing in the stock market.

One very important thing to take note of is that you have to be selective in what you read. Yes, you want to be reading, but reading the right books and feeding your mind with the kind of positive information is essential.

People who are experiencing situations in their lives want to be inspired, and one of the ways you can get this inspiration is by reading inspirational books. And can I tell you, there are so many of those kinds of books out there, you will not be able to read them all in your lifetime.

I challenge you today to go to your local library and get books to read. Remember we talked earlier about your 'Do Me Day', well, this is another perfect time to spend some quality time with yourself. You could take time to go to your local library and spend a couple of hours just reading your favourite books. And guess what, you might just ending up spending the entire day, as when you start reading a book and it is very interesting, you literally can't break away from it.

That's what reading does to you. This is also an opportunity to meet new people. Dr. Seuss says it perfectly, "The more that you read, the more things you will know. The more that you learn the more places you'll go."

Chapter 4.4 Story on Robert Hollis

"If someone is doing something that works, then why not do exactly what they tell you to do, believe in the faith of the process, and just work hard?" Robert Hollis was a car mechanic who lived in North Dakota with his family.

Although Robert worked so hard for his family to be financially alright, it was never like that. In fact, it got so bad that his family went on welfare for a while. He had to hide from his creditors because he had no money to pay them. Robert tried everything to ensure they were ok.

You see, some of the major differences between 'the have' and 'the have not' are that they never give up on their dreams, despite what their current situation is. They are persistent and they are always looking for the opportunity to get out of their challenging situations.

Robert got into internet marketing and started modelling his mentors. He believes those if you want to be your best at anything, find someone and model them. Yes, he believes in mentoring and coaching, but he strongly believes in people who have documented evidence of success. Robert Hollis says, "documentation beats conversation."

In 2011, Robert started his own company, called Unlimited Profits. He has made millions of dollars from this venture and is always looking for new and better ways to improve what he already has.

This is a real example of an individual for whom failure was never an option. He dreams big, sets his goals, and charts a course to achieving them. You should be inspired by Robert's story. Be encouraged by his journey from a humble beginning to being an influential figure, and a multimillionaire.

You too can use a mentor or a coach to help you through your situation. Email Sophia@OvercomingYourSetbacks.com or go to www.OvercomingYourSetbacks.com for more information on how I can be your coach.

Chapter 4.5 Connect With and Follow People of Influence

"Only through our connectedness to other can we really know and enhance the self. And only through working on the self can we begin to enhance the connectedness to others." Harriet Lerner

Did you know you are like five of the people you spend the most time with? Surrounding yourself with influential people does a lot for the mind. We all know that the mind is very powerful, and even though in reality you might not be like any of the influential persons you have connected with, you will start thinking like them. When this happens, providing that you are taking action, lots of opportunity will begin to come your way because the mind is telling the body that this is the direction you are taking and it has no choice but to follow.

There are some things you need to consider before actually following the persons you are interested in. You want to decide who exactly you want to follow, and the reason for following them. You will need to know how you will benefit from following them, and which social media you will use as your platform, as you will not be able to be on all the social media platforms that are out there. This would not be effective as you would have to be skipping from one social medium to the other.

Getting a glimpse into these people's lives allows you to get an idea of what they are thinking about, what they are doing, and just about any information you can get from them. Sometimes when you hear or see what successful people are doing, it inspires you to take action to improve your own life. We fail to understand that influential people have setbacks just like everyone else, but they use their experiences to motivate them to move forward.

Make today the day you start taking control of your life. Start by making the small changes which are necessary to move you forward to achieving your goals.

Chapter 4.6 Maintain The Right Attitude

Did you know that your attitude will determine how fast or slow you move forward? It is said that your attitude determines your altitude. And this statement is certainly true. Take a look at your own life and the different attitudes you have had over the years, and try to remember how they have affected you.

Looking back at my own life, I can stay that when my attitude is positive and I don't take criticism personally, I learn so much more, as I am able to react to things in a positive way even when it might have been done or said in a negative way.

In my own experience as a Police Instructor, I have personally seen how attitude affects my students in both a positive and a negative way. Consider the following 2 scenarios; I have changed their names for their privacy:

Terrence is an A student. Whenever I give exams and I provide feedback to Terrence, on areas in which he did not do well, he is not pleased. Instead he would say, "This is nothing much, you could have gotten me the full marks."

Remone is a B average student and whenever I gave him feedback from exams, his reaction is totally the opposite of Terence. Remone's response would be, "I know I can do better and you will see the difference on my next exam."

Have you noticed the difference in the two responses? Terrence might not maintain his A average for very long as he blames his instructor for his mistakes whilst Remone immediately provides a response that he will work on doing better on the next exam.

If you are responding to situations like Terrence did, even if the situation is different, , you need to consider changing your attitude as you only have control over what you do and how you react to people and situations. You have no control over people only yourself.

For the Remone types out there, kudos to you for maintaining the right attitude. Continue to improve on what you already have as this will certainly improve you overall.

Your attitude will definitely determine how your challenges affect you. Yes, it absolutely does affect everything you do so keep a positive attitude. Did you know that many persons are carrying around negative attitudes? And that's probably one of the main reasons why they are always in the sea of sameness and are not able to get on the island of individuality, as my mentor Raymond Aaron says.

Chapter 5 – Never Settle For Mediocrity

Chapter 5.1 Strive For Perfection

"Perfection is not attainable, but if we chase perfection we can catch excellence." Vince Lombardi

You're probably wondering why I am even talking about striving for perfection when we all know that no man or woman is perfect. It's impossible! So why bother to strive for perfection when we will never achieve it? Isn't this setting an unrealistic goal?

Striving for perfection motivates you to always do well. Even though, in reality, you cannot be perfect, striving for perfection gives you the drive to be better than you were before. It puts you in action mode to always do something to continue to be great at what you do. An unknown writer says "It's better to strive for perfection and fail, merely achieving greatness, than to strive for mediocrity and achieve it."

For those people who love sports, take the 100m Olympic record holder for example; Usain Bolt clocked 9.69 sec. in the 2008

Beijing Olympics and one would have thought it could not get better than that, but for Usain Bolt, there was much more left to come.

Usain continued to be motivated, trained harder and in the London 2012 Olympics, he did better than he did in 2008, clocking 9.63 sec. In addition, Usain Bolt currently holds the world record for the 100m at 9.58sec. and is probably putting in a lot of training to not only retain the coveted title at the 2016 Olympics but also to improve his time. However, there are other athletes who are working very hard to take Bolt's title away

This doesn't mean that if you fail you should be hard on yourself. Instead, be happy with yourself, knowing that you have set your goals high and have tried. You should now double your efforts, assess where you went wrong and implement new strategies to move you forward to achieving your goals.

Remember that failure is inevitable for all of us as human beings! As mentioned before, your failures should be seen as a learning opportunity; you can use them to guide you and make it easier for you to continue on your journey, as you are now able to avoid those first mistakes.

Remember it is very easy to settle for mediocrity, and that's why setting goals which force you to always take action to achieve them is important. Start setting goals which take you out of your comfort zone. Don't be afraid of failing; learn from your mistakes, remembering that this journey keeps you result driven. It propels you to constantly take action to achieve your goals. "Success is the result of perfection, hard work, learning from failure, loyalty, and persistence." Colin Powell

Chapter 5.2 Improve Your Brand

"Be a yardstick of quality. Some people aren't used to an environment where excellence is expected." Steve Jobs

In a previous chapter, we talked about building your brand. The image that the world has about you is very important as it will make or break you. We definitely have to always be cognizant of this and make great effort to improve what's already out there.

Your brand is how people see you when you are not present. As a matter of fact, even when people see you, they are always quick to google your name to see what comes up about you. We are all guilty of doing this, right? Jeff Bezos, founder and CEO of Amazon says, "Your brand is what people say about you when you are not in the room."

There are many things that we all can do to improve our personal brand. On your Facebook page, for example, you can do simple things to improve how people see you.

1. You should have the proper information in your about section of your Facebook page that you want people to know about you. So for example you should have a well-constructed summary of who are, basically telling your readers some of the things you want them to know about you. Remember, the aim of this should be building your personal brand.

2. You should make sure some kind of contact information is present. Again, you are trying to create and always improve the kind of personal brand people will want to associate with. No one wants be associated with a brand which has no value and will take away from what they have created for themselves.

3. You should be deliberate about the kind of posts you make. If you are posting photographs you want people to see, these should be pictures that enhance who you are, not the kind of posts that do nothing to improve your image. This should be a conscious decision. Again, people use those things to judge who you are. All your posts-- and I mean all of them -- should serve the purpose of improving your personal

brand, not demeaning you and taking away what you have worked so hard to create in the first place.

4. Another important area to think about is that if you want to have authority in your chosen field, it's usually prudent for you to put your qualifications. So there is an area under 'about' called 'education' where you could actually put the schools you have attended. This validates you as a professional in your area.

There are others things you can do to enhance your Facebook page. If you think you are not able to do this yourself, solicit the help of someone who is capable of making your page looks professional.

Your LinkedIn profile is one which people definitely look at to see what image you have, so again, it should always have a professional look. Whatever is on your profile should be a true picture of who you are. So let's look at what you can do to improve your LinkedIn profile!

1. Your profile photo should be a nice picture of you; and when I say nice I am sure you know what I mean. In that same area, you clearly state your name and exactly what you do (your job title), regardless of whether you're an entrepreneur or you work for someone else.

2. Under background, you are going to outline perfectly your experiences and your skills. If someone wants to see quickly what you have been doing, they should be able to see it at a glance. Remember that many people will not get the time to read your entire profile, so it's wise for you to summarize your experience in such a way that it gets noticed readily just from reading your background information.

3. Outline your experience in order of your most current work until you have highlighted your first work experience. And try not to have a break in your timeline; if you were not working for a specific time period, but you were volunteering, you should include that.

4. You need to highlight any special projects you might have worked on, in a way that your viewers would want to invite you to work on a similar project.

5. All the skills you possess should be outlined. In addition, when others in your network endorse your skills it strengthens what you say you can do, which in the long run improves your brand.

6. Another great way to build your brand is to have people recommend you. People who might have done some work

with you might recommend you without your asking; however, you may have to ask others to do this for you.

7. You should highlight your qualifications in order of the most current to the first qualification you obtained. This should include your short courses, as this also will strengthen what you already have.

There are so many other simple things you can do to improve your LinkedIn profile, such as say what your interests are by joining groups and have people who have influenced you on your profile.

I deliberately selected Facebook and LinkedIn as examples on how you can do simple things to improve your brand because most people are on social media and the internet is the quickest way to get any message out.

But again, another great way to improve your brand is to seriously consider writing a book. Writing a book gives you authority and it gives you the 'the wow' moments, as when people hear that an ordinary person writes a book, they are usually amazed that you were able to do that. And people are quicker to do business with you as your name is already out there. Do you see the power of being an author yet? It really does give you a buff.

You might be saying writing a book is not easy, and I agree with you. It's best if you get a mentor to guide the process for you as it takes more than just putting words on paper to get your book out. Go to www.OvercomingYourSetbacks.com for tips on how to get your book out.

Now that I have given you some key ways on how to improve your brand, do what you can do to improve what you already have, as this is what people see before they even see you. In fact, some might never see you in person.

Chapter 5.3 What's Your Value

"Your beliefs become your thoughts. Your thoughts become your words. Your words become your actions. Your actions become your habits. Your habits become your values. Your values become your destiny." Mahatma Ghandi

Now that we have looked at some of the things you can do to improve your brand, we will take a look at what your values are, and how they determine why you do the things you do.

Have you ever been in the lobby area of a company, and noticed a chart with all kind of fancy words about the company's core values? Well, like a company, we all have some values which we use to govern or guide what we do and basically how we act and make decisions both personally and in business.

It is important to know that our values cannot be 'in between;' they must be clear and definite. You must have taken a conscious decision based on some criteria to come up with those values you are guided by.

The people who fail to have that line of demarcation which they will not cross are sometimes left to think how did they get to the situation they find themselves in. Why? Because they have little or no core values which they are guided by! For example, people who are experiencing challenges, especially financial issues, might get caught up in things which later might make them ashamed of themselves if they are not mindful; in disbelief as to what they have done to gain money. The point I am making is that the lack of great values might come back to be your worst nightmare. It is said, if you do not stand for something, you will fall for anything

Many times people refuse to stand up for what they believe in because they want to fit in, and they are afraid of hanging on the fence by themselves. But guess what? It's better to uphold your values and be by yourself than being a part of a large crowd and compromising the values you have held so dear to you. Your values are yours; they might not be shared by anyone else but that is quite normal, as it is what helps to differentiate us. It is just what keeps you grounded and helps you to be true to yourself.

The values you hold connect you to people who share similar values, and this is very important, especially in business. Did you know that many business partners have disagreements because they get to the point where they realize that they are heading in different directions and most times they have no choice but to go their separate ways?

If you currently do not have core values which you use to guide what you do in life, start seriously thinking about getting some. This is very important in helping to build the kind of brand you want. There are great benefits to holding great values, as you will inspire others; and remember, your values are built over time; as the world evolves so do your values and beliefs.

Chapter 5.4 Matt Lloyd's Inspirational Story

Matt tells his inspirational story in his recently published book "Limitless". He moved from investing all his savings plus borrowed money in 2008 to now having a company generating more than $100,000,000 in revenue.

Matt started out by helping his parents on their farm. He saw the struggles of his parents in their business and he knew from early on that he wanted to earn big, but not the way his parents were doing it.

He moved on to university and soon realized that a degree was not what he wanted; instead he wanted to earn right away and a university degree was not going to give him the kind of income he was thinking about. He dropped out school to pursue a way he could make the kind of money he wanted.

Matt wanted to be a millionaire, but quickly he realized that to become that millionaire he had to break down his goals into smaller and more manageable goals to be able to accomplish them. As a consequence, he decided that he wanted to earn $100,000 first, within a year. He wrote down his goals and became obsessed with achieving them. He clearly charted a course on how he would realize his dreams.

Between the times he was making all those big plans, he was working for a menial salary and started a small business which was taking a lot out of him.

Matt picked up quickly that if he were to become a millionaire, he would have to be doing more than what he was currently doing. So he began searching for a new way out. He found a way of making money online by investing in an online marketing program with $2000. He later realized that high ticket items were making even more money for online marketers, hence, he invested all the money he had, which was $38,000. One would have thought this was a crazy idea.

However, when you believe in yourself and you are willing take action and be persistence with it, it's only a matter of time before you will begin to see success. . And that is what Matt did, he believed wholeheartedly in himself and his capabilities.

Can you believe he invested so much and for nine months no return and Matt continued to persevere? Yes, he stuck it out. How many of us could do that? Not many! He began to see little results of which he reinvested the little he was earning as he realized that if he was to see any great results this is what he would have to do.

 Matt was convinced that there was a huge market for high ticket products online and the company he had invested in did not have enough high ticket products and wasn't providing the support he needed. He began thinking how he could change that and his answer was starting his own company.. He founded the company which provides small business owners with online business education to move their businesses forward and partnering with affiliates to do this. MOBE as the company is called is now seeing over $100,000,000 in revenue and its owner Matt sees no ending to where his company will go.

Matt story is one of great inspiration to many including me. I continue to be encouraged by his account that so many people believed he was wasting his time and money. But he paid them little or no attention, as he knew that the actions he was taking now would have brought him a fortune in the future. Despite his temporary failure, he did not see them as that. Instead, it was the opportunity he got to learn from them and to implement better strategies to ensure he achieves his goals.

Placing your focus on the job at hand is very essential in succeeding. We see in Matt's story how important that is. He knew he could not focus on the negative influences like the people who were constantly telling him that he would not succeed.. Instead, he placed his energy on the end result and that was the success he was anxiously awaiting.

Do you now see the importance of thinking big? And not only to dream big but to take action to ensure your goals will be achieved. I hope you were inspired to start taking action right now.

Chapter 5.5 Maintain Integrity

"Real integrity is doing the right thing, knowing that nobody's going to know whether you did it or not." Oprah Winfrey

Integrity is that character trait which propels us to always do the things which are right. Remember we spoke at length about the values we hold? You see, the values we are guided by lead us to a life of integrity, but the reverse could also be true. If you are not guided by good morals and ethical principles then you will not care much about how you live, the kind of decisions you make and what people think about you.

People with integrity never have to question the decisions they make as their decisions are always based on the core values they are guided by.

For those people who are keen on building the kind of brand people can trust, having integrity is very important as they know that once they have lost their integrity, try as they may, they might not get it back. And even if they do rebuild their integrity at some point, there will be those people who will always be skeptical, based on the fact that they had compromised what they had before.

Living a life of integrity means that you are not really perturbed about whether you are being watched, as you will make sure that your integrity will never be questioned by doing what is right every time. For you, honesty is the hallmark of what you do and you need not say a word, as your action speaks volumes about your character and generally the kind of person you are. In fact, people will admire you more and will be inspired by you. As C.S. Lewis says perfectly, "Integrity is doing the right thing, even when no one is watching."

Did you know that having integrity is a conscious decision you make? Of course it is! People who do not develop integrity on their own will most times do what is right when they are being watched. It is easy for those people to do things which will cause their integrity to be questioned. So, it is important to always do the right things as you do not know who is watching without you knowing..

If you look carefully around you, there are people who will do anything for money, as this is what motivates them. This they do without any care of the consequences, or how it might affect their loved ones. In the words of renowned reggae singer Bob Marley, "The greatness of a man is not in how much wealth he acquires, but in his integrity and his ability to affect those around him positively."

You know what; we all can live our lives with great integrity, as it doesn't cost us anything to do so. Even when we are faced with what seems to be insurmountable challenges which we think we are not able to deal with, we should not compromise our integrity as this will make us lose out on opportunity.

People might want to give you the chance to break free of your setbacks through an opportunity, but because of the fact that they do not trust you, they don't even bother to offer it to you. So maintaining your integrity is of utmost importance as no amount of money in the world can purchase it. "If you don't have integrity, you have nothing. You can't buy it. You can have all the money in the world, but if you are not a moral and ethical person, you really have nothing." Henry Kravis

It's never too late to start doing what is right. Make a conscious decision to start living a life of integrity today. It's not difficult! Start by defining what your values are and since you are just starting this journey, you want to assess all the decisions you have made to ensure that your guiding principles were the foundation for your decision. Say to yourself, "Starting today, I am going to live a life that I will not have to question myself after any actions I have taken." Be your hardest critic.

Chapter 5.6 Be Better Than Yesterday

"If you continuously compete with others, you become bitter, but if you continuously compete with yourself, you become better." Unknown

Who do you compete with? Do you underestimate your abilities and constantly comparing yourself with others around you? Not only that, but you believe that they are better than you. Yes, you can use someone or something as a benchmark to be better at what you do. However, you should not compare or compete with others in the manner where you are consumed by it. This will keep you stuck, as you will become preoccupied by this rather than doing the things which will improve you.

Although we are constrained by the limited resources out there, we don't have to compete for anything, as enough is there for everyone. You can be anything you want to be. You can have anything you want to have. It all depends on how badly you want it and how much sacrifice you are willing to make to have what you want and to be what you want to be.

Of course, you should have a competitor but that competitor should definitely be you. You should be your greatest competitor. You should always aim to be better than you were before. You should set high standards for yourself. You should constantly measure where you are and your progress so much so that the slightest change there is, you are able to detect it.

Trying to compete with others makes you lose focus, and it totally distracts you from your goals and places your energy at a place where you will get no benefit. All this does is continue to drain you, and it makes you become envious and bitter to the point where you might no longer be able to see things clearly.

Can you see how all of this is to your own detriment? You repeat this cycle until you realize there is nothing left of you. The sad part about this is that your competitors might not even be cognizant of the fact that you are competing against them. And guess what, they are setting their goals and putting strategies in place to achieving their goals whilst your focus continues to be the same, competing and getting nowhere. How crazy is that? "Don't compare yourself with anyone in this world…if you do so, you are insulting yourself." Bill Gates

Constantly placing your focus and energy on trying to be better will certainly make you better. But don't even bother trying to be good at everything; you will be setting unrealistic goals which you will never be able to achieve.

Try to assess yourself to ascertain what your talents, strengths and weaknesses are. Chances are, you might never truly recognize all your talents as it is only when you are faced with varying challenges that you see some of your hidden talents come to the fore. When you are aware of your strengths and weaknesses, you are in a better position to put more focus on your areas of strengths to get even better at them.

We were all born with our unique differences. We have our own talents and abilities, and our own strengths and weaknesses. Find what yours are and perfect them; after all, only you can make you better than yesterday.

Chapter 7 – Think Big

Chapter 7.1 The Power of The Mind

"Whatever your mind can conceive and believe, it can achieve." Napoleon Hill.

Have you ever stopped to wonder why some people seem to be achieving and others are not? Well, some people are rich because they are from an affluent family. Others are rich in their minds until they begin to take action and see the manifestation of the riches they've always seen.

You have another set of people who are neither from an affluent family or rich in their minds. These people are usually the ones who cause their limiting beliefs to keep them stuck in their situation. They is no room for growth as the mind is clouded with negative perceptions. We have limiting beliefs which hinder us from demonstrating our true potential.

Our limiting beliefs prevent us from achieving our goals, no matter how hard we work to achieve them. They cripple our ability to see beyond today, as they fill our minds with fear instead of possibilities. "Don't limit yourself. Many people limit themselves to what they think they can do. You can go as far as your mind lets you. What you believe, remember, you can achieve." Mary Kay Ash

For some people thinking big comes natural. However, for many others a concerted effort has to be made to train the mind to think of all the possibilities and block out the negatives. I am sure when you want something, it's the thought that goes to you first; however, then you begin to think of all the reasons why you are not going to have it.

Guess what? The mind is so powerful that it gives you exactly what you want despite the fact that it might take time. Mind you, I am not saying that should only sit and think about what you want all day, waiting for it to come to you. Instead, I am saying position your mind on the things you want to achieve and set your goals, plan and implement strategies which will ensure that your goals will be achieved. So remember in the habit of thinking big to be mindful that your plan of action needs to be put in place.

Have you ever wanted to get something, whether it's a house, a car, or higher education, and the first thing your friends or family members say to you is, "Where will you get the money from?" Wow, what a nice way of crushing someone's dream.

Well, that is if you allow it to happen. It has happened to me over and over. I have invested heavily in myself in terms of academic pursuits, and a couple of years ago decided that I wanted to do my master's degree. I did not know where the money was coming from, but I applied anyways. The only thing I began to think about was getting my degree and nothing was going to stop me from achieving it. Thank God, I got accepted and completed my program without even having to borrow the money, with people looking on wondering how I managed to do that.

The point I am making is that when you want something, you have to want it so badly that you can't even see yourself without it. All of this permeates your mind, which gets your body in the motion of putting in the plans to ensure you will achieve whatever you want. "We become what we think about all day long." Ralph Waldo Emerson

I recommend you reading "Think and Grow Rich" by Napoleon Hill. It tells some powerful stories of persons who have aided their success by using the power of their minds.

We are the biggest obstacles in our own lives. We use our minds to prevent us from moving forward. In the words of Dennis Waitley, "The only limits on human achievement are self-imposed."

Of course, we all can be big thinkers. However, we have to first stop encouraging the negativity in our minds. The fears which we sometimes have cripple our ability to think big. Fear gets us in the habit of procrastinating and making excuses when it doesn't want us to move forward, so we have to take control of our life.

Take control of the things you think about. Take control of the negative emotions which come with life stresses. You can do it; remember, many persons have done it before, many persons are doing now, and many will continue to do it. Train your mind to be positive. You can consciously make the decision to do this; use your mind to your advantage, because if you fail to do this, it is going to be used against you. Sad, but it is reality of how the mind works.

The mind is extremely powerful. Don't be too hard on yourself though, if you are not able to take full control of your mind overnight. This is an ongoing process; just continue to be focused and practice, practice. And instead of beating up on yourself, get into the habit of always finding ways to help with training your mind. Remember that worrying about your problems will not solve anything, instead focus on solving the problem and, with time, you will be on your way.

The power of the mind is nicely outlined in this poem taken from 'Think And Grow Rich' – Napoleon Hill

"If you think you are beaten, you are,
 If you think you dare not, you don't,
 If you like to win, but you think you can't,
 It is almost certain you won't.

If you think you'll lose, you're lost,
For out in the world we find,
Success begins with a fellow's will,
It's all in the state of mind.

If you think you're outclassed, you are,
You've got to think high to rise,
You've got to be sure of yourself before
You can ever win a prize.

Life's battles don't always go
To the stronger or faster man,
But soon or late the man who wins
Is the man who thinks he can!"

Make it your daily habit to practice using the mind to think positive. It is not going to be easy, but with time and great effort you will master the habit of thinking big. "Think big. Believe big. Act big. And the result will be big." Positivelife.com

Take some time to do this short exercise.

1. What are you thinking about right now? (write it down)
2. Start thinking about something that you thought you could never have done. (make it big)

Chapter 6.2 Let Your Imagination Go Wild

"Logic will get you from A to B. Imagination will take you everywhere." Albert Einstein

We have just looked at the power of the mind, and how our minds can be used to serve us but can also be used against us. I am sure you prefer to use your mind to think bigger than you can imagine whilst you actively put plans in place to ensure those big dreams will become a reality one day. Now we are going to look at how our imagination works.

Do you know that there is no limit to what we can imagine? Our imagination goes way beyond what we are able to fathom; if we let it, that is. However, many of us intentionally or unintentionally put a limit to what we can imagine.

It is our imagination which allows us to come up with great ideas. The power of our imagination contributes significantly to our successes, as with this, we can form mental pictures of what exactly we want to achieve. Of course, it doesn't stop there as we need faith; there can be no doubt in our minds that we will achieve.

What about our feelings? They also aid our imagination. Consider, for example, that you want to buy a house in the countryside. Start imagining yourself inhaling the fresh air from being in the countryside, see yourself looking and touching your house, visualize the exact colour you want, and smell the awesome aroma coming from your kitchen.

You see, your imagination allows you to have what you want before you actually get it. Sounds weird, right? But that's how powerful our imagination can be. What it also does is make it seem so real that we have no option but to start putting plans in place to have it, even when it seems farfetched to everyone else. If this action is repeated, it begins to attract the right people and the right opportunities, which will bring our imagination closer to becoming a reality. In the words of Tony Robbins, "Your life is controlled by what you focus on." Make it count!

Always maintain a positive attitude, keep the desire for your imagination to become a reality as strong as possible, and avoid negative people. Remembering that you are like 5 of the people you spend the most time with, so you definitely have to be mindful.

Yes, be mindful of your feelings, whether they are positive or negative, the things you think about and as I said earlier the people you surround yourself with. Make a conscious effort to make sure your imagination goes wild, and do it as often as possible. Your 'Do Me Day' is a perfect time to start training you mind to be imaginative. Outside of your 'Do Me Day', make time to practice, as we all know practice makes us get better at whatever it is we are trying to accomplish.

Do you now start seeing the power of your imagination? Or you might have known the power of it before but you just needed to be reminded. Take all the limiting beliefs from your mind and allow your true potential to be demonstrated. You were born with greatness in you.

Take advantage of the power you have, put plans in action and before you know it those wild imaginations might just become a reality for you. Remember that the moment the imagination brings you an idea, it is within your reach to achieve it. "If you can imagine it, you can achieve it. If you can dream it, you can become it." William Arthur Ward

Chapter 6.3 Relieve Yourself of Limiting Beliefs

"People often become what they believe themselves to be. If I believe I cannot do something, it makes me incapable of doing it. But when I believe I can, then I acquire the ability to do it even if I didn't have it in the beginning." Mohandas Gandhi

You have come a far way with me and for that I say thank you. We have looked at imagination and how powerful it is. We've seen that once we allow our minds to go wild and there's an idea, it can become a reality if we intensify our desire whilst putting the necessary plans in place. Let's now look at relieving yourself of your limiting beliefs.

Have you ever been looking for a job and even though you have applied you tell yourself that you are not going to get the job as many applicants are more qualified with more experience than you? Well, you have defeated the purpose of applying for the job in the first place.

That is your limiting belief. You believe that you are not capable enough to get the job and so that's the result you will get. Individuals who believe in themselves do not limit their potential. That is one of the main differences between people who are successful and people who are not. "You are what you are by what you believe." Oprah Winfrey.

Do you know that some of our limiting beliefs might actually have some basis? For example you want to start a business and you have no money for capital and you are saying that you will not be able to start the business until you get the money. This is indeed a fact, and to remedy the problem you could try getting a loan from family, friends or even a financial institution.

The same goes for people who are experiencing some kind of setback in their lives. You sometimes put a limit to your ability to come up with solutions to your problems. Once you have done that, it becomes very difficult for you to overcome your challenges. It basically cripples your progress and leaves you in a situation which seems all doom and gloom.

Your limiting beliefs diminish your possibilities. In your mind, there is no way out and you refuse to even try again as it has been deeply fixed in your thoughts, which you then demonstrate in your behaviour.

All is not lost though, as you can consciously rid yourself of your limiting beliefs with practice. To start the process of diminishing your limiting beliefs and replacing them with affirmation of your greatness you have to first be able to identify them. You have to also ascertain what triggers your limiting beliefs. Once you have identified these, then you can begin to replace them with positive self-talk as they are probably the reasons you are not accomplishing your goals. Go to www.OvercomingYourSetbacks.com for more tips to relieve your limiting beliefs.

Again, it is very important to understand that your limiting beliefs are not real; they are exactly what they are, beliefs which restrict you from moving forward to achieving your goals.

So, take action, however minute. The important thing is to get started, as we all know taking the first step is usually the most difficult. Maxwell Maltz postulates perfectly, "Within you right now is the power to do things you never dreamed possible. This power becomes available to you just as soon as you can change your beliefs."

Chapter 6.4 Be Focused

"Stay focused, go after your dreams and keep moving toward your goals." LL Cool J

Are you focused on the things which will move you forward? Staying focused on anything important is usually not the easiest thing to do, as we are constantly bombarded with all kinds of distractions, such as work, family and the various other things we have to do. The things you focus on can benefit you, but conversely, they can be of detriment to you.

I just blamed all the distractions we have in our lives as the excuse not to stay focused. But that's not good enough, as we will always have those things in our lives; that's just the reality. So, it is really not a good reason not to be focused as we have choices. It always in our best interest to prioritize, as this allows us to do the things which are more important first.

Remember we talked earlier about taking responsibility for our actions and the lack thereof. This is no different; you definitely need to take responsibility and take the next step by figuring out what is preventing you from staying focused. When you do this, you will have to decide how it is you are going to manage those distractions to be able to put place your focus on the important things that you want to achieve.

With anything you do in life, a balance is very important, so put strategies in place which will help you to stay focused on those little things which will move you forward. The measures you put in place should be such that they motivate and keep you accountable for actions which you should take to achieving your goals. And remember if you fail to do a planned task, don't be too hard on yourself; just get on it immediately and get it done. As the saying goes, better doing late than not doing it at all.

You can revisit setting goals in our previous chapter to see how you can stay focused by making your goals more manageable by breaking them down into smaller tasks. If you implement those strategies, staying focused on the important things will not be so difficult after all. Need I remind you, don't forget to reward yourself for your accomplishments, however small they are.

"Successful people maintain a positive focus in life no matter what is going on around them. They stay focused on their past successes rather than their past failures, and on the next action steps they need to take to get them closer to the fulfillment of their goals rather than all the other distractions that life presents to them." Jack Canfield

Chapter 6.5 Always Be Thankful

"Gratitude unlocks the fullness of life. It turns what we have into enough, and more. It turns denial into acceptance, chaos to order, confusion to clarity. It can turn a meal into a feast, a house into a home, a stranger into a friend." Melody Beattie

How recently have you stopped to thank your supreme being, or even a person who has done a kind deed for you? Being thankful is one of those things which we seldom do. Most of us wait for those special times of year to show our gratitude and appreciation to others. We spend so much time complaining about what we don't have instead of giving thanks. The fact that we have life is enough to be thankful. Of course once we have life, there are always possibilities, and sometimes if we only know what others are experiencing we would be even more grateful for what we have and the ability we have to set goals and work at achieving them.

The story was told of a man who thought all hope was gone and he decided that there was not much to live for anymore so he decided to take his life. He had one ripe banana, climbed into the tree to take his life but decided to have the banana first. as After he ate the banana he threw the peel down, and a man passing picked it up and ate it, because he was so hungry. The despondent man saw what the other man did and climbed down from the tree as he realized that his problems were not so bad after all.

There are always others who are experiencing more problems than you think you have, and one would never know, as rather than focusing on the problem, they put all their attention on finding solutions to their situation. And in the meantime they thank God for what He has done and what He will continue to do.

There are many different ways to be thankful. You can do this through praying, you can do this through a thankfulness journal and just about anything you want to do, to be thankful. Thankfulness allows blessings to be bestowed on you and puts you in a place of happiness. "It's not happy people who are thankful, it's thankful people who are happy." Curiano.com

Thankfulness should not only go to the higher being but to individuals who have helped you along your journey. A simple thank you to someone for a deed does a lot, not only for you who is showing gratitude but for the other person as well. You could use a card to show your gratitude or even the other media which the internet has now made available to us.

Think about a time when someone did a good deed for you and you told the person thank you. How did it made you feel, and what did it do for the other person? Gratitude brings a sense of joy and appreciation to the people with whom who are involved. I have certainly felt that way and I am sure that at some point in time you have felt that way too.

Do you know that just saying thank you to someone has some benefits? A study done by the University of Kentucky in 2012 showed that participants who were more thankful had a higher ranking on the gratitude scale. It showed that even when people behaved unkindly to individuals who were more grateful they were less likely to retaliate in a negative manner. So you see it's not so bad after all to say thank you. There are actually some benefits to be had from it.

Start showing more gratitude today. Make it a habit to be thankful for what you have in possession and don't be afraid or too proud to say the words to someone who has done some kind deed for you, however small it might be. It says something about you and it does something for the person you are saying thank you to. Suze Orman says, "When you are grateful - when you can see what you have - you unlock blessings to flow in your life."

Chapter 7 – Fulfill Your Purpose

Chapter 7.1 What's Your Big Why?

"Efforts and courage are not enough without purpose and direction." John F. Kennedy

Every person here on earth was born for a purpose. You were born for a reason and despite the fact that you have been experiencing difficulties it does not negate your God-given purpose in life.

Have you ever wondered about your purpose in life? To find your given purpose, one has to look deeply in themselves to find that drive, to ascertain that reason why you do the things you do. It might be that you had to go through your situation to have a testimony so that others could be inspired by your story.

Your big why helps to differentiate you from everyone else. Knowing your big why helps you to focus on the things which are important to you. To be able to know your big why, you have to first ascertain what makes you motivated. What are your morals and values? Why do you do the things you do? What are your goals? What are you passionate about? These are just some of the questions you need to ask yourself to discover your big why.

Your big why is definitely one of the important components of your life. It is certainly your purpose, and the sooner you are able to identify what this is, the closer you are to living your passion. And when you commit to living your passion, you make a conscious decision to live a meaningful and happy life. When you are aware of your big why and you think about it, you should immediately experience a lot of joy, peace and sheer excitement. You see, this is why your big why should be about you and not anyone else as this will bring about unhappiness.

It's you that you are putting forward; one of my professors, Tony Gifford, would often tell his students, 'You Inc.' is that part of you that the world sees, so you better make it good as that is what determines your success. Your big why is definitely your personal brand.

Knowing your big why makes it easier for you accomplish your goals, as you already know why you do the things you do. It gives you a purpose to move forward and sets the foundation needed for greater success. If for some reason you don't know your big why, there are simple questions that you can answer, to ascertain what it is. These questions I will outline below.

1. What motivates you?
2. What's your passion?
3. Why do you do the things you do?
4. What's your mission?

Of course nothing in life is really easy, so no matter what you are doing, you will become frustrated. One of the great benefits of your big why is that when you are overwhelmed and you start thinking about your big why, you should feel a sense of purpose and a renewed spirit to get the tasks done. Our big whys are what keep us motivated. They let us persevere through our good times and more so our most challenging times.

Failure is just never an option for people who know what their big whys are, as they have a reason to wake up each and every day. They are no longer victims reacting to their circumstances, but are in total control.

Challenge yourself today to ascertain what exactly your big why is. You will observe soon that it is one of the key ingredients to achieving your goals as it keeps you disciplined and motivated. Your big why gives you the impetus to take control of your life, which makes overcoming obstacles easier. "Discipline is the bridge between goals and accomplishment." Jim Rohn

Chapter 7.2 Find Your Passion

"There is no passion to be found playing small - in settling for a life that is less than the one you are capable of living." Nelson Mandela

Have you ever done something you were unhappy about but you did it anyway? Or, you might have started doing something that you enjoyed doing and as time progressed you realized that just thinking about it made you frustrated. Well, I believe that we all have experienced this situation at some time or another.

And can I tell you that it has happened to me. I was doing the same job for a long time and just getting out of bed and thinking where I had to go in the next hour or so made me literally angry. Looking back at that job, I now realized that it was not the job in itself but the system that was in place.

Guess what, I took action! I am from the Caribbean, I had family, lots of responsibility and I decided it was time to make my move. I decided that I would enrol in an overseas academic program to get an international qualification to make me more marketable. The program was very expensive, but that was not enough excuse for me not to take action.

I told my family I was leaving my job and going to Canada to study. I got accepted in the Global Business Management program at Humber Business School and I left my home, where we have warm weather all year round, to go to cold Canada to study. Crazy me right, I thought so too!

The point I am trying to get across is that when you realize that what you are currently doing makes you unhappy, take action. Despite the challenges which you might face when you do, still don't allow it to deter you; take action anyway. It is obvious that you are not passionate about it, hence the unhappiness and the frustration you feel day in day out. Of course, it's always great when you make your impressive plans.

However, sometimes you have to take immediate action, which forces you to give some urgency to your situation and find that which makes you happy.

In this situation, you might not see a clear plan of action or a straightforward vision to move you forward, but over time you should find the things that you naturally love to do begin to give you hints as to where to start to find your passion. Start giving them serious thought; you might just find that's where your love lies.

A lot of the time, we have failed to take action because the job we have pays the bills, and even though we are so unhappy we become complacent and don't even bother to search for our passion. You can find that which you love to do. Yes, you need to find your passion.

You should not make money your primary consideration when searching for your passion; however, often when you do the things you are passionate about, they end up making you a lot of money in the process. Sometimes you work long hours but it never feels like that, as you are doing what you love to do.

I challenge you today, as you read through the pages of this chapter, to go in search of your passion, and when you do find it, begin the process of taking action. In time you'll see the true result.

Finding and following your passion is the key to start fulfilling your purpose as it motivates you and gives you a reason for living, in addition to giving you the drive to demonstrate your true potential. T. D. Jakes says it perfectly in these words, "It is your passion that empowers you to be able to do that thing you were created to do."

Take a little time to respond to the following.

1. What's your passion?
2. Are you currently doing your passion?
3. If no, why not?
4. Start searching for your passion.

Chapter 7.3 Serve Others

"You have not lived today until you have done something for someone who can never repay you." John Bunyan

So we have looked at how finding and following our passion helps to bring about some happiness and rid ourselves of frustration. We talked about how doing what we love to do is part of the process of fulfilling our purpose in life. Now we are going to look at how important it is to serve others.

Serving others is one of those things we all want to be able to do at some point in time in our lives, although many people never get around to helping other people outside of their circle. The reasons sometimes given are:

1. I don't have the time
2. I don't have enough money

3. I am too young or
4. I am too old couple with other excuses

There's never a better time than now to start serving others. Serving others is necessary and it is an important part of who we are as people. Sometimes because of our circumstances, like the ones I've mentioned before, we do not believe we are capable of helping. But that's the time when we are to make the effort to help others. And this is certainly not a difficult task.

You can help others by volunteering at a not-for-profit organization like the Red Cross, Hear The Children's Cry, or the many others out there helping humanity. They are always looking for people to help them as they are usually experiencing financial constraints. You might want to look even closer in your actual neighbourhood, as there might be an elderly person in your community who needs help. You could go grocery shopping for the person, do the person's lawn and just about anything the person requires of you to make them comfortable.

Did you know that serving others brings fulfillment? Yes it does! When you provide that help and you know that the person has benefitted and is grateful, it definitely makes you happy and you want to do it again and again. There are so many other benefits to be had when you serve others.

Serving others helps you to build on existing skills and learn new ones, in addition to learning about other people's culture. Consider, for example, that you are volunteering at a homeless shelter and usually you are great at oral communication. Serving at the shelter builds on what you have because you have to interact with these people to provide the service they require. You might learn a thing or two about diversity as you might be dealing with people who are not like you in every sense of the word. And just talking with them gives you a peak into their culture, beliefs and their personality! Serving others opens up a window of opportunity to learning new things, and it stretches your capabilities. Just don't put a limit on what can be had from your volunteering experience.

Helping others might be just what you need to help you with your own challenging situation. When you do to others without looking back for anything it brings blessing to your life. We all talk about karma and most of the time use it only in the negative way. Someone does something bad to you and you hope karma gives it back to them. The same is true when you do a good deed for someone; karma will reward you, if not now then in the near future.

Have you noticed so many of the influential people around the world are giving back to society in their own way? Some are giving away a large percentage of their fortune to different organizations, two of whom are Warren Buffet and Bill Gates. Many of them have started foundations which are helping so many people around the world, like the Anthony Robbins Foundation, which is helping to feed millions of less fortunate among us.

Kudos to all those who are helping in their own way, whether it's through giving of time or money! But did you know that you don't have to physically do a good deed? Instead, you could give your support by donating cash or kind to those organizations that provide services to the less fortunate. That is just another great way of giving back!

Do all the good you can by serving others. If you have never done it before, start making some calls to your local not-for-profit organizations and see what help they require which you might be able to provide for them. Remembering that one of our purposes in life is to help others! Mother Teresa puts this nicely, "At the end of life we will not be judged by how many diplomas we have received how much money we have made, how many great things we have done. We will be judged by 'I was hungry, and you gave me something to eat, I was naked and you clothed me. I was homeless, and you took me in.'"

Chapter 7.4 Be An Inspiration

In your actions inspire others to dream more, learn more, do more and become more, you are a leader." John Quincy Adams

At some point in time in your life, you must have had even one person who you admired a lot and tried to emulate as much as possible. For me, that person was Mrs. Manning from Kellits Primary School; for me she was one of those people who never saw the negative in anyone.

We all know grade 6 age students can act up sometimes as this is the time when puberty starts setting in; we would behave inappropriately in class and Mrs. Manning would tell us, "There is good in you and you need to start demonstrating that for your own good."

For many other teachers, those behaviours definitely would have warranted a day or two of detention, or some other kind of punishment. Mrs. Manning inspired students to be their best and played a significant role in many students' lives in our early years at primary/elementary school. She was the kind of person who led by good examples, and even though she's not here anymore, I can still hear those encouraging words coming from her on a daily basis.

So if you have had that kind of person around you, try to identify and adopt some of those good qualities and start being the one to inspire others. Inspiring others is not difficult at all, especially with the advancement in technology and the influx of so many platforms such as Facebook, LinkedIn, Instagram and the many others which are popping up every so often.

Have you ever noticed on one or more of the social media platforms you use that almost every day you can see some inspiring posts from individuals? I have seen it and what it does for me is makes me starts thinking about my own life and what I could do to change those areas which need to be adjusted. Those inspirational posts propel you to take action.

Do you see how important it is for you to make your personal brand one that inspires? When others are inspired by your actions and just how you portray yourself, it gives you authority and people will start believing in you.

From this, people might just start requesting you to give talks at different events and pay you to do something which in essence was never the main focus initially. This is just one of the ways it works when you build that brand which inspires people to take action.

You might be saying "Yes, I can do some of the things you have mentioned, but how do I get started?" And my response to you would be to start making small changes to how you live your life. By that I mean, if you are a person who never exercises much, you could start an exercise program and follow through with it; if you are a person who gives no attention to eating healthily, well, start making healthy eating choices. People around you will start seeing the changes and want to engage you to see what's up. When you are making these small changes, be passionate about your new habits and maintain the right attitude too, as the people seeing your changes might just be inspired to make the changes in their lives as well.

Do you know that what seem to be minute changes might just mean a lot to another person? Yes, it might just be, as starting healthy habits is not the easiest thing to do for many people and the fact you might have had your own struggles, before you got the courage to start, might propel others to take action.

Another great way of inspiring others is to tell your story. Of course, we all have our own individual stories which when told will encourage others that they are not alone in their struggles. You can tell your story by writing a book, you can start a blog or just about any way you see it fitting to tell others about your comeback from your setbacks.

You have a compelling story, despite the fact that you are experiencing your challenges. People are always curious to know about other people's experiences. The fact that you are not allowing your current situation to hinder or stifle your ambition puts you in a better place to realize your dreams! Find creative ways of writing about your situation and how you have triumphed; put it out there so other people can be inspired by it. There are individuals out there who are probably experiencing or have experienced your situation and would be encouraged to know that they are not alone. Don't wait on the next year or five years' time, or when you retire; tell your story now.

Remember in inspiring others, you have to keep yourself motivated. Be guided by good morals and values and never allow your integrity to be questioned as when you lose it, you might never be able to reclaim it.

Chapter 7.5 What Legacy Do You Want To Leave?

"All good men and women must take responsibility to create legacies that will take the next generation to a level we could only imagine." Jim Rohn

Have you ever thought of how you want to be remembered when you are gone? This is something that we do not give much consideration to, but it is nice to create the kind of legacy you want to leave behind.

For many, their legacy will be their children and the lives of people they might have touched in their close circle. For others, their legacy has reached the world and they will be talked about for many generations to come. Some of these people are Mother Teresa and Martin Luther King Jr.

Some of those people who have made significant contributions which that touched the world did not actually set out to do it. It just happened that they did what they loved to do and it ended up affecting some change to society. For others, creating a legacy has been on their minds since they can remember, hence, they deliberately set out to create the kind of legacy they want to be remembered by.

Of course, many of us will not make those significant contributions that will change the world. However, it is important that you try to live a life that will touch even the lives of your family members and friends. What I mean, being a mother is a significant job so you want to be the kind of mom who always looks after your children's wellbeing. It is usually so nice when your children can say "My mom is the best" or

"My dad was so a great he can never be replaced." Make a significant contribution in your small corner and you will have done something significant.

There are so many little things which you can do to create the kind of legacy you want. Again, this will not affect a world change, but you will have left a lasting memory among your loved ones. So one of the things you want to do is to be there for your family members and friends. Show them love and support them in every way you can, providing this does not compromise your morals and values. You can extend this to people you come in contact with. Say something motivating to your employees, your coworkers and just about anyone you think could use an encouraging word.

It's so nice when you support causes of your friends and relatives and they do the same for you. In the long run it's more support for each cause which they can never get enough support for. Of course, supporting a cause usually makes a fulfilling life as you are giving back to society in your own way. You are helping someone in need in one way or another, which is a blessing. This could be giving of your time and/or providing monetary support which so many of those organizations need. This is just another great way of helping the less fortunate.

If you have not yet started to provide any kind of support to anyone in need, you might want to give it some consideration because so many people and organizations out there would welcome some kind of help from you.

Remember, one the first things you can do for yourself is find your passion. Your passion is what fuels you to greatness and opens the windows of opportunity for you to do so many things you probably didn't even think you could do. Your passion motivates and gives you purpose in life; it propels you to take action and in the process of doing all of this, you are creating a legacy without even knowing it. Remember that your legacy is fuelled from your years of being on this earth, so consciously live a life of purpose, one which you and your loved ones can be proud of!

Your Steps Forward

"If your view of reality is not supportive, is not positive, is not charging you with energy and joy and zest each day, it is time to change what you are paying attention to. It is time to change your focus. It is time to change your very definition of what reality is, what your life is, what your future will be." Brendon Burchard

If you are at this point with me, you have come a long way, and I thank you for staying the course. As I close the pages of this book, I am using the opportunity to reiterate the fact that we all have obstacles and challenges which we must overcome. These are inevitable; we just cannot escape them. However, we should always use our challenges and failures as an opportunity to learn something new.

To start the journey of getting past your hurdles, there are some things you need to do. First, you have to establish where you are. Acknowledge where you are and take responsibility for your situation before you can truly chart a course to move forward. When you do this, you are able to take the appropriate action to help you achieve your goals and live the rewarding life you were meant to live.

The victor is deep inside of you. If only you look deep enough, you will discover it. Search yourself, find it and be the person you were meant to be. Nobody says the process of getting past your hurdles is easy; still, you have to be determined and decide that falling victim to your circumstances will never be an option.

Remember that the goals you set should allow you to measure your progress as you move along. You should set realistic goals and put a time to when you want to accomplish those goals. To make your goals manageable it is recommended that you break them down into smaller more workable goals like your short-, medium- and long-term goals. And make sure that you write your goals down.

Of course to get your goals accomplished within your scheduled time, it is usually prudent for you to be accountable to someone. That person could be anyone who is capable of playing this role. It could be your mentor or coach, or even yourself. As much as possible, you should write your goals down as each time you look them, it serves as a reminder that there's work to be done.

Investing in yourself is key to moving forward. Look at what you have, including your strengths and weaknesses, and see what you can do to improve as a person. You can go back to school; you can utilize the internet to teach yourself basically anything you wish to learn. You can start building a personal brand as this will help you greatly.

Your setbacks can prevent you from realizing your dreams if you permit it. Remember, the key to moving beyond this is to surround yourself with inspiring people. Get a mentor, family, friends and support groups that can provide that support when you feel like giving up. Do a lot of self-talk, read inspiring books and fill your mind with positive information which will help you to fight the negatives.

Maintain the right attitude as this determines how you see things. Remember it is said that your attitude determines your altitude. If you think you are experiencing challenges that you believe you are not able to deal with by yourself go to www.OvercomingYourSetbacks.com and get the help which is necessary to help you live the fulfilled life you were born to live.

Think big, and I mean real big! Never doubt the power of the mind. Constantly set your mind on the things you so desperately want to achieve. In all of this, set your goals, plan and implement strategies which will ensure that your dreams will become a reality in the shortest possible time. Once you have rid yourself of your limiting beliefs, the sky is the limit in terms of what you can accomplish.

Fulfill your purpose. You were born to do so. Ascertain your big why and your passion as, once you have knowledge of this, it makes it easier for you to find the drive to get things done. And of course, this gives you motivation to take action to turn your situation around.

So now you have read my book, and you think you are not able to deal with your challenges by yourself. Of course, you are not alone! Get a competent coach or mentor to work with you, as this will make it easier for you. If you believe you were inspired by my book, feel free to make contact with me at www.OvercomingYourSetbacks.com as I would be more than happy to work with you as your coach to ensure you are at the point where you are living the life you were meant to live.

You have two options. You can be inspired and motivated by your situation or you can allow yourself to be restricted and marred by your situation. I hope, like me, you will choose to be motivated to take action.

As I close these pages, I leave these inspiring words with you from Albert Einstein: "Whatever situation you are in your life, your mind, your thoughts, your philosophy, your thoughts got you there. To get out of that situation you gotta reach out to people, different thoughts, different psychology, different philosophy."

www.ingramcontent.com/pod-product-compliance
Lightning Source LLC
Chambersburg PA
CBHW070920270326
41927CB00011B/2661